D0013483

DATE DUE

CREATION REGAINED

Biblical Basics
for a
Reformational Worldview

BY
ALBERT M. WOLTERS

GRAND RAPIDS, MICHIGAN
WILLIAM B. EERDMANS PUBLISHING COMPANY

To Alice,
sine qua non

Copyright © 1985 by Wm. B. Eerdmans Publishing Co.
255 Jefferson Ave. S.E., Grand Rapids, Mich. 49503
All rights reserved
Printed in the United States of America

Reprinted, July 1988

Library of Congress Cataloging in Publication Data

Wolters, Albert M.
  Creation regained.

  1. Cosmology, Biblical.   2. Creation.   3. Fall of man.
4. Redemption.   I. Title.
BS651.W65   1985   230'.57   84-26019

ISBN 0-8028-0043-2

CONTENTS

Acknowledgments

This little book arises out of my teaching at the Institute for Christian Studies in Toronto, Canada, and owes a great deal to my interaction with its Junior Members, whom I hereby thank most cordially. It would never have achieved final written form without the support and help of Bob and Mark VanderVennen, to whom I also here express my sincere gratitude. The coaxings of the father were well seconded by coaching of the son. What I owe to my wife, Alice, is best expressed by dedicating this work to her with all my love.

Author's Note

For those readers who may be interested in pursuing the issues raised in these pages, I would recommend *All of Life Redeemed: Biblical Insight for Daily Obedience*, by Bradshaw Frey, et al. (Jordon Station, Ont.: Paideia Press, 1983), and *The Transforming Vision*, by Richard Middleton and Brian Walsh (Downer's Grove, Ill.: InterVarsity Press, 1984), two fine introductory works. For more advanced study I would recommend Herman Dooyeweerd's classic *Roots of Western Culture: Pagan, Secular, and Christian Options* (Toronto: Wedge, 1979).

CREATION
REGAINED

1

What Is a Worldview?

This book is an attempt to spell out the content of a biblical worldview and its significance for our lives as we seek to be obedient to the Scriptures. The ideas that make up this worldview are not original with me. They come from a long tradition of Christian reflection on the Scriptures and our overall perspective on the world, a tradition rooted in the Scriptures themselves. It has had as some of its most prominent representatives the Church Fathers Irenaeus and Augustine, and the Reformers Tyndale and Calvin.

This scripturally informed worldview is sometimes called "reformational," after the Protestant Reformation, which discovered afresh the biblical teaching concerning the depth and scope of sin and redemption. The desire to live by Scripture alone, rather than Scripture alongside of tradition, is a hallmark of the Reformers. We follow their path in this emphasis as well as in wanting an ongoing reformation, in wanting to be re-formed by the Scriptures continuously (see Acts 17:11, Rom. 12:2) rather than living by unexamined traditions.

Reformational reflection on worldview has taken distinctive shape as it has moved into the twentieth century, something that can be seen specifically in the work of such Dutch leaders as Abraham Kuyper, Herman Bavinck, Herman Dooyeweerd, and D. H. T. Vollenhoven. Their contributions to a more profound and articulate understanding of the biblical worldview have come through theology, philosophy, and other academic disciplines, and especially through cultural and social action arising from a deep desire to be obedient to the Scriptures in all areas of life and service.

The term *worldview* came into the English language as a trans-

lation of the German *Weltanschauung*. It has the advantage of being
clearly distinct from "philosophy" (at least in German usage) and
of being less cumbersome than the phrase "world-and- life view,"
which was favored by the Dutch neo-Calvinists (probably following
a usage made popular by the German philosopher Dilthey). An
acceptable synonym is "life perspective" or "confessional vision."
We may also speak more vaguely about the whole of a person's
"principles" or "ideals." A Marxist would call it an "ideology"; the
most prevalent label in the secular social sciences today is probably
"system of values." These terms are less than acceptable because the
terms themselves have connotations of determinism and relativism
that betray an unacceptable worldview.

For our purposes, *worldview* will be defined as "the comprehensive
framework of one's basic beliefs about things." Let us take a closer
look at the elements of this definition.

First of all, "things" is a deliberately vague term that refers to
anything about which it is possible to have a belief. I am taking it
in the most general sense imaginable, as encompassing the world,
human life in general, the meaning of suffering, the value of education, social morality, and the importance of the family. Even God
can in this sense be said to be included among the "things" about
which we have basic beliefs.

Second, a worldview is a matter of one's *beliefs*. Beliefs are different from feelings or opinions because they make a "cognitive
claim"—that is, a claim to some kind of knowledge. I may say, for
example, that I "believe" that education is the road to human hap-
piness. That means that I am asserting something about the way
things are, what the case is. I am willing to defend that belief with
arguments. Feelings do not lay claim to knowledge, nor can they
be argued.

Beliefs are not opinions or hypotheses either. To be sure, we
sometimes use the word *belief* in that sort of weakened sense ("It is
my belief that Johnny will come home late again tonight"), but I
am here using the word *belief* in the sense of "credo," a *committed*
belief, something that I am willing not only to argue, but also to
defend or promote with the outlay of money or the endurance of
hardship. For example, it may be my belief that freedom of speech
is an inalienable right in human society, or that no one should
impose his or her religion on someone else. To hold a belief may

call for sacrifice on my part, or the endurance of scorn or abuse if it is an unpopular or unorthodox belief—say, that prisons should punish as well as rehabilitate, or that free enterprise is the scourge of our society. All such beliefs are examples of what goes into a worldview. It has to do with one's *convictions*.

Third, it is important to note that worldviews have to do with *basic* beliefs about things. They have to do with the ultimate questions we are confronted with; they involve matters of general principle. I might say that I have a secure belief that the Yankees won the 1956 World Series, secure to the extent that I am willing to make a large bet on it, but that kind of belief is not the sort that constitutes a worldview. It is different in the case of profound moral issues: Can violence ever be right? Are there constant norms for human life? Is there a point to suffering? Do we survive death?

Finally, the basic beliefs one holds about things tend to form a *framework* or *pattern*; they hang together in a certain way. That is why humanists often speak of a "system of values." All of us recognize, to some degree at least, that we must be consistent in our views if we want to be taken seriously. We do not adopt an arbitrary set of basic beliefs that has no coherence or semblance of consistency. Certain basic beliefs clash with others. For example, the belief in marriage as an ordinance of God does not comport well with the idea of easy divorce. A conviction that movies and the theater are essentially "worldly amusements" is not very consonant with the ideal of a Christian reformation of the arts. An optimistic belief in historical progress is hard to harmonize with a belief in the depravity of man.

This is not to say that worldviews are never internally inconsistent—many are (in fact, an inconsistency may be one of the most interesting things about a worldview)—but it remains true that the more significant feature of worldviews is their tendency toward pattern and coherence; even their inconsistencies tend to fall into clearly recognizable patterns. Moreover, most people will not admit to an inconsistency in their own worldview even when it is very obvious to others.

It has been assumed in our discussion so far that everyone has a worldview of some kind. Is this in fact the case? Certainly it is true that most people would not have an answer if they were asked what their worldview is, and matters would only be made worse if they were asked about the framework of their basic beliefs about things. Yet their basic beliefs emerge quickly enough when they are faced with practical emergencies, current political issues, or convictions that clash with their own. How do they react to military conscription, for example? What is their response to evangelism or the counterculture, to pacifism or communism? What words of condolence do they offer at a graveside? Whom do they blame for inflation? What are their views on abortion, capital punishment, discipline in child- rearing, homosexuality, racial segregation, artificial insemination, film censorship, extramarital sex, and the like? All of these issues trigger responses that provide indications of a person's worldview by suggesting certain patterns ("conservative" and "progressive" being very rough and unreliable patterns that most people recognize). In general, therefore, everyone has a worldview, however inarticulate he or she may be in expressing it. Having a worldview is simply part of being an adult human being.

What role does a worldview play in our lives? The answer to this, I believe, is that our worldview functions as *a guide to our life*. A worldview, even when it is half unconscious and unarticulated, functions like a compass or a road map. It orients us in the world at large, gives us a sense of what is up and what is down, what is right and what is wrong in the confusion of events and phenomena that confronts us. Our worldview shapes, to a significant degree, the way we assess the events, issues, and structures of our civilization and our times. It allows us to "place" or "situate" the various phenomena that come into our purview. Of course, other factors play a role in this orientation process (psychological or economic self-interest, for example), but these other factors do not eliminate the guiding role of one's worldview; they often exert their influence precisely *via* our life-perspective.

One of the unique characteristics of human beings is that we cannot do without the kind of orientation and guidance that a worldview gives. We need guidance because we are inescapably creatures with responsibility who by nature are incapable of holding purely arbitrary opinions or making entirely unprincipled decisions. We need some creed to live by, some map by which to chart our course. The need for a guiding perspective is basic to human life, perhaps more basic than food or sex.

It is not only our views and arguments that are decisively affected by our worldview, but all of the specific decisions we are called upon to make as well. When the going gets rough in a marriage, is divorce an option? When taxation is unjust, do you cheat on your tax forms? Should crime be punished? Will you fire an employee as soon as it is economically advantageous to do so? Will you get involved in politics? Will you discourage your son or daughter from becoming an artist? The decisions you make on these and many other issues are guided by your worldview. Disputes about them often involve a clash of basic life- perspectives.

Again, we have to admit that there can be inconsistency here: not only might we hold to conflicting beliefs, but sometimes we might fail to act in harmony with the beliefs we hold. This is a fact about our everyday experience that we must all acknowledge. But does this mean that our worldview therefore does not have the guiding role that we are ascribing to it? Not necessarily. A ship can be diverted from its course by a storm and still be heading for its destination. It is the overall pattern that counts, the fact that the helmsman does everything possible to stay on course. If your action is out of tune with your beliefs, you tend to change either your actions or your beliefs. You cannot maintain your integrity (or your mental health) for long if you make no effort to resolve the conflict.

This view of the relation of our worldview to our conduct is disputed by many thinkers. Marxists, for example, hold that what really guides our behavior are not beliefs but class interests. Many psychologists look on worldviews as more guided than guiding, as rationalizations for behavior that is really controlled by the dynamics of our emotional life. Other psychologists contend that our actions are basically conditioned by physical stimuli coming from our environment. It would be foolish to dismiss the evidence these thinkers adduce to substantiate their views. It is in fact true that human behavior is very complex and includes such matters as class interests, conditioning, and the influence of repressed feelings. The question is what constitutes the *overriding* and *decisive* factor in accounting for the pattern of human action. The way we answer that question depends on our view of the essential nature of humankind: it is itself a matter of our worldview.

From a Christian point of view, we must say that belief is a decisive factor in our lives even though our professed beliefs may be at variance with the beliefs that are actually operative in our lives.

It is the command of the gospel that we live our lives in conformity with the beliefs taught in the Scriptures. That we often fail to live up to this command does not invalidate the fact that we can and ought to live according to our beliefs.

What, then, is the relationship of worldview to Scripture? The Christian answer to this question is clear: our worldview must be shaped and tested by Scripture. It can legitimately guide our lives only if it is scriptural. This means that in the matter of worldview there is a significant gulf between those who accept this Scripture as God's word and those who do not. It also means that Christians must constantly check their worldview beliefs against the Scriptures, because failing that there will be a powerful inclination to appropriate many of our beliefs, even basic ones, from a culture that has been secularizing at an accelerating rate for generations. A good part of the purpose of this book is to offer help in the process of reforming our worldview to conform more closely to the teaching of Scripture.

As Christians we confess that the Scriptures have the authority of God, which is supreme over everything else—over public opinion, over education, over child-rearing, over the media, and in short over all the powerful agencies in our culture by which our worldview is constantly being shaped. However, since all these agencies in our culture deliberately ignore, and in fact usually reject outright, the supreme authority of Scripture, there is considerable pressure on Christians to restrict their recognition of the authority of Scripture to the area of the church, theology, and private morality—an area that has become basically irrelevant to the direction of culture and society as a whole. That pressure, though, is itself the fruit of a secular worldview, and must be resisted by Christians with all the resources at their disposal. The fundamental resources are the Scriptures themselves.

The Scriptures are many things to the Christian, but central to their purpose is *instruction*. There is no passage in Scripture that cannot teach us something about God and his relationship to us. We must approach the Scriptures as students, particularly when we begin to think critically about our own worldview. "Everything that was written in the past was written to teach us," says Paul of the Old Testament Scriptures (Rom. 15:4), and the same applies to the New Testament. That is why the concept of "sound doctrine" is so

central in the apostolic witness—not doctrine in the sense of academic theology, but as practical instruction in the life-and-death
realities of our walk in the covenant with God. It is by means of
that kind of teaching that the steadfastness and encouragement the
Scriptures bring will enable us, as Paul goes on to point out in the
same passage, not to despair but to hang on to our hope in Christ.
That is also involved in what Paul calls the "renewal of our minds"
(Rom. 12:2). We need that renewal if we are to discern what God's
will is in the full range of our lives—"his good, pleasing and perfect
will." Testing our worldview against Scripture and revising it accordingly is part of the renewal of the mind.

This emphasis on scriptural teaching is, of course, a fundamental
aspect of the Christian religion. All varieties of Christians, in spite
of all their differences, agree on this point in some form or other.
Yet it is necessary to stress it again with reference to the question
of our worldview because almost all branches of the Christian church
also agree that the teaching of Scripture is basically a matter of
theology and personal morality, a private sector labeled "sacred"
and "religious," marked off from the much broader range of human
affairs labeled "secular." The Scriptures, according to this view,
should certainly shape our theology (including our "theological ethics") but are at best only indirectly and tangentially related to such
secular affairs as politics, art, and scholarship: the Bible teaches us
a church-view and a God- view, not a worldview.

This is a dangerous error. To be sure, we must be taught by
Scripture on such matters as baptism, prayer, election, and the
church, but Scripture speaks centrally to *everything* in our life and
world, including technology and economics and science. The scope
of biblical teaching includes such ordinary "secular" matters as labor,
social groups, and education. Unless such matters are approached
in terms of a worldview based squarely on such central scriptural
categories as creation, sin, and redemption, our assessment of these
supposedly nonreligious dimensions of our lives will likely be dominated instead by one of the competing worldviews of the secularized
West. Consequently, it is essential to relate the basic concepts of
"biblical theology" to our worldview—or rather to understand these
basic concepts as *constituting* a worldview. In a certain sense the plea
being made here for a biblical worldview is simply an appeal to the
believer to take the Bible and its teaching seriously for the totality

of our civilization *right now* and not to relegate it to some optional area called "religion."

All of this raises the question of the relationship of what I have been calling "worldview" to theology and philosophy. This is a subject of some confusion, since in common parlance any comprehensive perspective on things that appeals to the authority of the Bible is called "theology," and any such perspective that appeals instead to the authority of reason is called "philosophy." The trouble with this way of speaking is that it fails to make a distinction between the life-perspective every human being has by virtue of being human and the specialized academic disciplines that are taught by professors of theology and philosophy. Moreover, it makes the mistaken assumption that theology cannot be pagan or humanistic and that philosophy cannot be biblical. The difference between Christian and non-Christian cannot so easily be divided between two academic disciplines.

Theology and philosophy are specialized fields of inquiry that not everyone can engage in. They require special skills, a certain kind of intelligence, and a fair amount of education. They are fields for trained experts. This is not to say that they are closed to the intelligent layman; it simply means that laymen are at a distinct disadvantage in them, just as they are in medical science, economics, and such nonacademic special fields as high finance and international diplomacy. In all these fields there are professionals—men and women who are specialists in the area. Theology and philosophy are no exceptions.

But a worldview is a quite different matter. You do not need degrees or special skills to have a perspective on life. Biblical wisdom or sound doctrine does not increase with advanced theological training. If it did, the prophets and apostles, not to mention Jesus himself, would have been quite deficient compared to today's bright young theologians fresh out of graduate school. Academic brilliance is something quite different from wisdom and common sense—and a worldview is a matter of wisdom and common sense, whether biblical or unbiblical.

Without attempting to define precisely the nature of "science" and "theory" (which in this context we can assume to be synonymous), it can be said that philosophy and theology, as academic disciplines, are scientific and theoretical, whereas a worldview is not. A worldview is a matter of the shared everyday experience of humankind, an inescapable component of all human knowing, and as such it is nonscientific, or rather (since scientific knowing is always dependent on the intuitive knowing of our everyday experience) *prescientific*, in nature. It belongs to an order of cognition more basic than that of science or theory. Just as aesthetics presupposes some innate sense of the beautiful and legal theory presupposes a fundamental notion of justice, so theology and philosophy presuppose a pretheoretical perspective on the world. They give a scientific elaboration of a worldview.

In general, then, we can say that worldview, philosophy, and theology are alike in being comprehensive in scope, but that they are unlike in that a worldview is prescientific, whereas philosophy and theology are scientific. The distinction between philosophy and theology can perhaps be made more clear if we introduce two key concepts: "structure" and "direction." Philosophy can be described as that comprehensive (totality-oriented) scientific discipline which focuses on the *structure* of things—that is, on the unity and diversity of creational givens. Theology (i.e., Christian systematic theology), on the other hand, can be said to be that comprehensive (totality-oriented) scientific discipline which focuses on the *direction* of things— that is, on the evil that infects the world and the cure that can save it. Christian philosophy looks at creation in the light of the basic categories of the Bible; Christian theology looks at the Bible in the light of the basic categories of creation. A worldview, by contrast, is equally concerned with both structural and directional questions. It does not yet have the differentiation of focus characteristic of the comprehensive scientific disciplines.

There is a good deal that can be said about these distinctions, especially about the distinction between structure and direction, but that will have to wait until a later point in our discussion. At the moment we are only touching on it briefly to clarify the relationship between the three comprehensive ways of understanding the world.

Now that we have a general idea of what a worldview is, it remains for us to address the question of what is distinctive about the reformational worldview. What characteristic features distinguish it from other worldviews, both those pagan or humanistic and those Christian?

We must begin by coming to terms with the fact that there are different Christian worldviews, even within the mainstream of historic Christian orthodoxy. There is a sense, of course, in which all orthodox Christian churches (which we will in this context understand to be those Christian churches that accept the so-called ecumenical creeds of the early church) share a good deal of basic biblical teaching. They all accept the Bible as God's Word, believe in a transcendent Creator who made all things, confess that the human predicament is due to sin and that Jesus Christ has come to atone for that sin and redeem mankind from its curse, affirm that God is personal and triune, that Christ is both divine and human, and so on. We must not minimize the extent to which Eastern Orthodox, Roman Catholic, and various kinds of Protestant traditions share in the same biblical heritage and confession.

Nevertheless, we are well aware of the deep divisions within the Christian church. These divisions reflect differences of worldview as well as differences of theology in the strict sense of the word. I would like briefly to identify the basic difference between a reformational worldview and other Christian worldviews.

One way of seeing this difference is to use the basic definition of the Christian faith given by Herman Bavinck: "God the Father has reconciled His created but fallen world through the death of His Son, and renews it into a Kingdom of God by His Spirit." The reformational worldview takes all the key terms in this ecumenical trinitarian confession in a universal, all-encompassing sense. The terms "reconciled," "created," "fallen," "world," "renews," and "Kingdom of God" are held to be cosmic in scope. In principle, nothing apart from God himself falls outside the range of these foundational realities of biblical religion.

All other Christian worldviews, by contrast, restrict the scope of each of these terms in one way or other. Each is understood to apply to only one delimited area of the universe of our experience, usually named the "religious" or "sacred" realm. Everything falling outside this delimited area is called the "worldly," or "secular," or "natural," or "profane" realm. All of these "two-realm" theories, as they are called, are variations of a basically *dualistic* worldview, as opposed to the *integral* perspective of the reformational worldview, which does not accept a distinction between sacred and secular "realms" in the cosmos.

That is one way of explaining the distinctiveness of the reformational worldview. Another way is to say that its characteristic features are organized around the central insight that "grace restores nature"—that is, the redemption in Jesus Christ means the *restoration* of an original good creation. (By *nature* I mean "created reality" in these contexts.) In other words, redemption is *re-creation*. If we look at this more closely, we can see that this basic affirmation really involves three fundamental dimensions: the original good creation, the perversion of that creation through sin, and the restoration of that creation in Christ. It is plain how central the doctrine of creation becomes in such a view, since the whole point of salvation is then to salvage a sin-disrupted creation. In nonreformational worldviews, however, grace includes something in addition to nature, with the result that salvation is something basically "noncreational," supercreational, or even anticreational. In such perspectives, whatever it is that Christ brings over and above creation belongs to the sacred realm, while the original creation constitutes the secular realm.

In the next three chapters we will look at the three basic biblical categories of creation, fall, and redemption. Thus far we have talked rather abstractly about the reformational worldview in order to place it in the broader context of Christian worldviews as a whole. Now it is time to become more specific, relating the reformational worldview to both the central themes of Scripture and the basic realities of our cultural and societal experience.

2

Creation

The Law of Creation

The word *creation* has a double meaning. When we talk about "the story of creation" we are referring to God's activity of making the world; when we speak of "the beauties of creation" we are referring to the created order as the resulting *cosmos* (the Greek word for "ornament," "beautiful arrangement"). Creating activity and created order ought not to be confused.

Nevertheless, though distinct, these two senses of *creation* are closely related. This is true not only in the sense that creation as God's creating activity took place long ago, "in the beginning," and that creation as created order has been with us ever since. That is true enough, but if we do not say more, we will be sailing into the treacherous waters of deism, the heresy that we can dispense with God's creating activity once the clock of the cosmos has been wound up and set ticking. The fact is that the same Creator God and the same sovereign power that called the cosmos into existence in the beginning has *kept* that cosmos in existence from moment to moment to this very day. "Long ago by God's word the heavens existed and the earth was formed out of water and with water," writes the apostle Peter, referring to the creation story in Genesis 1, but *"by the same word* the present heavens and earth are reserved for fire, being kept" (2 Pet. 3:5, 7). God's commanding omnipotence, by which he makes all things to be what they are, is the same in the beginning of creation and in every moment of the history of creation. This is what theologians have meant when they have written that it is difficult, if not impossible, to make a decisive distinction between "creation" and "providence" as works of God. God's daily work of preserving and governing the world cannot be separated from his act of calling the world into existence. "To make" and "to rule" are all of a piece in God's vocabulary. From day to day every detail of our creaturely existence (the very hairs on our head) continues to be constituted by the "Let there be's" of the sovereign will of the Creator. The created order is in every instant unimaginable without the creating activity of God. The two are correlate: both senses of *creation* belong inseparably together.

In considering the biblical idea of creation, therefore, we must not for a moment lose sight of the Creator's sovereign activity in originating, upholding, guiding, and ruling his world. In fact, if we want to do justice to the Bible's teaching of God's sovereignty over all, we must give as the very definition of *creation*, "the correlation of the sovereign activity of the Creator and the created order."

This raises a kind of terminological difficulty that is familiar to the student of biblical theology and dogmatics. What term shall we use to describe the acts of God's sovereignty by which he constitutes and upholds the totality of reality? The Bible uses many different words; it speaks of God's power, of his breath, of his word, of his rule, of his hand, of his plan, of his will, of his call, of his decree, of his ordinances and statutes. All of these terms express some aspect of what we have been calling the sovereign activity to which created reality corresponds, but none of them captures the whole. Is there one term that we can select to stand for the whole of this activity, to facilitate our discussion of an overall biblical worldview? Or should we make up a new technical term, not found in the Scriptures themselves, the way theologians have coined such terms as *trinity*, *sacrament*, and *omnipotence*?

For reasons that will become clearer as we go on, we are going to use the word *law* to stand for the totality of God's ordaining acts toward the cosmos. It would have been tempting to use the world *creation* itself, but we have seen how unserviceable this word is— too broad because it also commonly refers to created things, and too narrow because in our normal usage (unlike that of the Bible) it excludes God's acts of providence. Another good biblical word is *wisdom*, but in the Scriptures this refers much more often to human wisdom. An equivalent from the theological tradition might be "the revealed will of God" or God's *opera ad extra*, but each of these is fraught with misleading connotations. *Law* has the advantage not only of being a central biblical word but also of focusing attention on God as *sovereign*, as absolute Lord and King. Law is the manifestation of God's sovereignty in creation. The Creator lays down the law for all his creatures; he rules the world by fiat; all things live and move and have their being by his sovereign legislative decree. "For he spoke, and it came to be; he commanded, and it stood firm" (Ps. 33:9).

In using *law* in this sense, we must be careful to keep in mind that we are referring to law as it relates to *creation*, God's design for the world and human life from the beginning. This is to be distinguished from God's saving acts of grace in *re-creation*, though these are connected most intimately with law in creation. In other words, in this connection, too, we must distinguish between *law* and *gospel*, although they must not be pitted against each other.

Law in this sense, even when it is distinguished from the works of redemption, is very rich and variegated in its extension. It encompasses a great variety of things, phenomena, relations, and principles—in fact it encompasses the whole range of created reality. It is not our concern to catalogue these now (it is the job of philosophy to make an inventory of the variety), but there are two pairs of distinctions to be made within the broad category of law that must claim our attention immediately: the distinction between laws of nature and norms, and the distinction between general and particular laws.

There are two ways in which God imposes his law on the cosmos, two ways in which his will is done on earth as in heaven. He does it either directly, without mediation, or indirectly, through the involvement of human responsibility. Just as a human sovereign does certain things himself, but gives orders to his subordinates for other things, so with God himself. He put the planets in their orbits, makes the seasons come and go at the proper time, makes seeds grow and animals reproduce, but entrusts to mankind the tasks of making tools, doing justice, producing art, and pursuing scholarship. In other words, God's rule of law is immediate in the nonhuman realm but mediate in culture and society. In the human realm men and women become coworkers with God; as creatures made in God's image they too have a kind of lordship over the earth, are God's viceroys in creation.

Corresponding with these two ways of ruling are two kinds of law: laws of nature and norms. We are all familiar with the laws of nature, the regular order in the realm of physical things, of plants and of animals. These include the laws of gravity, motion, thermodynamics, photosynthesis, and heredity— all the "natural laws" discovered by physics, chemistry, biology, and the other "natural sciences." We are not so familiar with, or feel less sure about, God's laws for culture and society, which we call *norms*. To be sure, we recognize norms for interpersonal relationships, but we are hesitant about any norms for societal institutions as such, or for something so mundane as agriculture. Yet both Scripture and experience teach us that God's will must be discerned here too, that the Creator is sovereign over the state as much as he is over the animal kingdom, that he is Lord over agriculture as much as he is over energy exchanges. God's statutes and ordinances are over everything, certainly not excluding the wide domain of human affairs.

There is, however, a crucial difference between the laws of nature and norms. In speaking of the "stormy winds that do his bidding" (Ps. 148:8), the psalmist does not ascribe responsibility to the wind. The wind cannot help but obey. But human beings do have responsibility: we are held to account for the way we execute God's commandments, and we are liable to punishment if we do not execute them at all. Norms are complex. They can be violated in any number of ways, and they also leave a good deal to the resourcefulness and responsible imagination of the human being who is called to implement them. The command "Be just" must be applied to many different and complex human situations, nor is it always easy to determine in any given situation what justice requires. Yet it is our uniquely human task to put into concrete practice the requirements of the norm for justice. A falling stone has no comparable task in obeying the law of gravity, nor does an eagle in observing God's ordinances for raising its young. The stone obeys necessarily, the eagle responds instinctively, but a person must exercise personal responsibility: we are called to *positivize* the norm, to apply it to specific situations in our lives. All of human life, in all its vast array of cultural, societal, and personal relationships, is *normed* in this sense. The almighty Creator lays claim to it all; the universal Sovereign lays down his laws for it all; the absolute King requires his will to be discerned in it all.

To the secularized Western mind, the distinction between laws of nature and norms is so great that they appear not to be different varieties of the same category but different categories altogether. Many people are willing enough to speak of "laws" of nature (unless they are somewhat sophisticated, in which case they reject the term *laws* as too metaphysical, and speak of "models" instead) but have long since abandoned the idea of given norms for human behavior. At best they will speak of "values," a term that speaks volumes about the attempt of contemporary humanity to emancipate itself from all divine imperatives. To see laws of nature and norms as continuous with each other is a confusion of facts and values to the modern mind, a mixing up of the "is" and the "ought."

The modern Western mind is exceptional in this view, however. For all of the divergences among worldviews throughout the history of mankind—primitive or "higher," cultic or philosophical, pagan or biblical—nearly all worldviews are united in their belief in a divine world order that lays down the law for both the natural and the human realms. They have called that order many different things—*Tao* in the Far East, *Maat* in ancient Egypt, *Ananke* and *Moira* in Greek religion, *Logos* or form in Greek philosophy, wisdom in the Bible—but they all have in common the idea of an order to which both mankind and nature are subject. Yet, among them, biblical religion is unique in proclaiming a God who is not himself subject to, but as Creator has *posited*, the world order. The Bible, too, mentions the ordinances for nature and mankind in one breath:

He sends his command to the earth;
　　his word runs swiftly.
He spreads the snow like wool
　　and scatters the frost like ashes.
He hurls down his hail like pebbles.
　　Who can withstand his icy blast?
He sends his word, and melts them;
　　he stirs up his breezes, and the waters flow.
He has revealed his word to Jacob,
　　his laws and decrees to Israel.
He has done this for no other nation;
　　they do not know his laws.
Praise the Lord.

(Ps. 147:15-20)

There is no essential difference, it would seem, between God's word of command to snow and ice and his command to his people. Whether laws of nature or norms, they belong to his universal law for all creation.

A second distinction exists within creation law between general and particular, and it too can be illustrated from the passage just quoted. When the psalmist speaks of God's laws and decrees he clearly has in mind general rules, such as the Ten Commandments, which apply to a wide variety of circumstances. "You shall not murder" is not a command addressed by God exclusively to a particular person at a particular time and place ("Don't you kill that Egyptian, Moses!") but a law that holds *generally* for all people, in all times, and in all places. Even when a law or decree is more restricted in scope (e.g., "If a man breaks the Sabbath, he shall be stoned"), it nevertheless holds for *all* cases that fit the description, for as long as the legislation is in effect. The case is different, however, when the psalmist sings, "He sends his word, and melts them." In describing the Creator's sovereignty over nature, the poet pictures a thaw in winter (or perhaps the breaking of spring) and says, in effect, "God commanded that thaw, right then and there." The commandment of God is here quite particular, restricted to a specific time and place. It is as particular as the falling of one hair from my head, or of one sparrow from the sky, and that too is part of God's plan.

It is clear that the distinction between general and particular laws cuts across the distinction between laws of nature and norms. Laws of nature are usually understood to be universally valid, and yet individual natural occurrences involve unique features that are not reducible to the aspect of universal regularity. These unique features, too, are according to the providential will of God. And it is plain that norms too are universally valid, as in the case of God's imperatives to be just, to be faithful, to be stewardly, and so on. But God's will for human beings is not only general but also particular, touching us in what has traditionally been designated "calling" or "guidance." What we have called the "law" of creation, therefore, is both compelling (laws of nature) and appealing (norms), and the range of its validity can be both sweeping (general) and individualized (particular).

Two further remarks should be added about the general/particular

distinction. The first is that the word *law* has to be stretched somewhat from its ordinary meaning to accommodate the sense of "particular command." We do not usually use *law* in this sense, although
it is clearly very close in meaning to "command" and does bear this
wider meaning in expressions such as "his word is law." The second
is that the universal validity of God's law reflects his *constancy* in
dealing with his creatures. We must not understand universal validity as entailing the absolute sense of a metaphysical determinism
divorced from God's personal characteristic of faithfulness or trust-
worthiness (Hebrew *'emet*, "truth") in his dealings with others.
Though God may surprise and amaze us (and often does; we then
speak of "miracles"), this does not suggest that we cannot depend
on him; on the contrary, it underscores his utter reliability. In other
words, there is no tension between the universal and particular in
God's law.

The Word of God in Creation

In the Scriptures there is a close connection between God's "word"
and his law. The word of the Sovereign is law, and it is often quite
appropriate to translate the Hebrew *dabar* ("word") as "command"
when it refers to God's speaking. The phrase "stormy wind fulfilling
his bidding" (Ps. 148:8), for example, is the NIV revision of the
more literal "fulfilling his *word*" of the King James Version. Since
the expression "word of God" and its equivalents ("word of the
Lord," "your word") play a key role in certain passages of Scripture
dealing with creation, we should take a closer look at the half-dozen
passages concerned.

In order to do that, we must first consider the creation account
in Genesis 1, which seems to be the background of many if not all
of the word-of-God passages that refer to creation. We are all familiar with the majestic opening words of that chapter, "In the
beginning God created the heavens and the earth," and we realize
(though it took a clash with pagan philosophy to find a precise
theological formulation) that these words refer to a *creatio ex nihilo*,
a creation out of nothing. The early church had to counter certain
heresies that claimed that God worked with eternal, preexistent,
uncreated matter as his raw material, the way a human craftsman
does, and the way the divine Craftsman or Demiurge made the

world in Plato's *Timaeus*. We don't always realize, however, that God's creative acts in the subsequent six days of creation do presuppose an already created "earth," unformed, empty, and dark, and that the subsequent sovereign "Let there be's" of the Creator establish a variety of creational distinctions (light/darkness, above/below the firmament, sea/dry land, etc.) *within* that already created but initially unfinished earthly realm. In other words, we cannot strictly speak of *creatio ex nihilo* in the case of God's creative fiats in the six days. Instead, creation here has the character of *elaborating* and *completing* the unformed state of earthly reality. This is what the theologians have called *creatio secunda*, as distinct from the first and primordial creation of heaven and earth out of nothing, the *creatio prima*. This illustrates again how difficult it is to make a sharp and clear distinction between creation and providence.

We should also note, in passing, that the Scriptures here use both "heaven" and "earth" in broad and narrow senses. It is the broad sense that is meant in the opening statement that God created heaven and earth. The focus of the narrative then immediately turns to the earth ("Now the *earth* was formless and empty . . ."), and heaven in that original sense (presumably heaven as the place of God's throne and the home of the angels) is no longer spoken of. However, in going on to describe the divisions that God commands to take place within "earth" in the broad sense—what we might call "earthly reality" to avoid confusion—the story gives the name "heaven" to the firmament as well (v. 8; cf. NIV), and the name "earth" to the dry land as well (v. 10). "Heaven," then, can mean both the realm of God's throne and the angels, and also the realm of sun, moon, and stars (the "sky"). And "earth" can mean both earthly reality (in the sense of the created cosmos outside of God's dwelling place) and the dry land as distinct from the seas. This is of significance in considering man's dominion over the "earth." A second passing remark is that the expression "formless and empty" in verse 2 does not describe a chaos—that is, the antithesis of cosmos (the currently prevalent interpretation, which draws on Babylonian parallels); rather, it describes the first step toward the order of the earthly cosmos, something like the preliminary rough sketch of the artist, which is later filled in with color and detail, or like the bare frame of a house before it is finished and furnished.

The point is that there is no distortion of God's good creation before man's sin: *formless* means "unformed," not "deformed."

For our discussion of the "word" in creation, this means that God's creative pronouncements—"Let there be light," "Let there be a firmament," and so on (eight times in all)—refer to *creatio secunda*, the elaboration and furnishing of the earthly realm into a beautiful cosmos. This is what the psalmist means when he says, "By the word of the Lord were the heavens made" (Ps. 33:6), referring to the second word of command, "Let there be a firmament." No doubt it is also what the apostle Peter is alluding to when he writes the words we quoted earlier: "Long ago by God's word the heavens existed and the earth was formed out of water and with water" (2 Pet. 3:5), calling to mind also the third creational fiat: "Let the water under the sky be gathered to one place, and let dry ground appear." "Secondary creation" also seems to be what the author of the letter to the Hebrews has in mind when he says, "By faith we understand that the universe was fashioned by the word of God" (Heb. 11:3, NEB), where the word translated "fashioned" is the same word used elsewhere of the potter's activity in making a lump of clay into an earthenware vessel (cf. Rom. 9:22). By his word of command God "works up" the unformed earth into a masterpiece of the craftsman's art.

We might be tempted to follow certain theologians and use "word of God" for what we have been calling God's creation "law." Certainly it is true that the Scriptures use "word" to refer not only to creation, but also to the upholding (Heb. 1:3) and governing (Ps. 147:18 and 148:8) of God's providence. Nevertheless, such a usage would be unwise because in by far the most cases the phrase "word of God" is used in Scripture to refer to God's message of sin and grace expressed in human language, and in theological literature it has long been used to refer to the Scriptures themselves. To give it yet another standard theological meaning would only cause confusion.

The most important reason for this digression on "word of God" as one of the Bible's terms for the law of creation is the connection made in the prologue of John's Gospel between creation and Christ as the eternal Word: "In the beginning was the Word, and the Word was with God, and the Word was God. He was with God in the beginning. Through him all things were made; without him nothing

was made that has been made." The repeated phrase "in the beginning" clearly points to creation as described in Genesis 1, when
"all things were made." The apostle John here teaches us (as the
other apostles had before him—see Col. 1:16 and Heb. 1:2 and
2:10) that creation took place "through" Christ. There is a sense
in which Christ is the "mediator of creation." Moreover, by giving
Christ the title "Word," he suggests an intimate connection between
Christ "through whom" and the word of God "by which" the universe was fashioned. He seems, therefore, to be alluding specifically
to the fiats of Genesis 1, but it is not clear whether he distinguishes
them from the *creatio ex nihilo* of its opening verse. (The word translated "was made" and "were made" does not make the matter any
clearer; it means simply "became" or "came into being," which
could easily refer to creation in either sense.) Whether or not John
has the distinction in mind, however, we can at least see from his
words that Christ is at the very center of God's act of creation.

Furthermore, the New Testament also clearly teaches that Christ
is intimately involved in the *preservation* of creation. Not only is it
true that "all things were created by him," but "in him all things
hold together" (Col. 1:16, 17). He is the Son of God, "through
whom he made the universe," but he is also "sustaining all things
by his powerful word" (Heb. 1:2, 3). The all-powerful upholding
word of God is also the word of his Son. In short, Christ is intimately present in the whole range of what we are calling the law
of creation. He is the mediator of both creation and re-creation.

The Scope of Creation

Everything we have said thus far has served to underscore the centrality in Scripture of God's sovereign law over all of creation—or
rather of the integral place that law has in the very concept of
creation, biblically conceived. The idea of a creation law will be
our point of departure and constant point of reference in the rest
of our discussion of creation.

If we understand creation to be the correlation of law and cosmos
(or of law and "subject," since the whole created order is *subject* to
the overarching law of God), then it is immediately clear that "creation" has a scope much broader than common usage gives it. Usually when we speak of creation we have in mind the realities

investigated by the natural sciences—the structure of the atom, the movements of the solar system, the life cycle of a plant, the building instinct of a beaver. That is the sort of thing that comes to mind when we speak of the "wonders of creation." Alternatively, we may think of a majestic snow-capped mountain or the vast expanses of the starry sky. Our understanding of creation is usually restricted to the physical realm. The same understanding is reflected in the name "Creation Research Society," an association largely concerned with a scriptural approach to such fields as physics, geology, astronomy, and biology. The disciplines of sociology, aesthetics, political science, and economics fall outside the Society's area of investigations.

We will not make such a distinction if we understand creation in terms of a law-subject correlation. God's ordinances also extend to the structures of society, to the world of art, to business and commerce. Human civilization is *normed* throughout. Everywhere we discover limits and proprieties, standards and criteria: in every field of human affairs there are right and wrong ways of doing things. There is nothing in human life that does not belong to the created order. Everything we are and do is thoroughly *creaturely*.

There are a few places in Scripture where the basic confession of God's creational sovereignty is specifically applied to such non-physical realities. According to Paul, marriage is among the things "which God created to be received with thanksgiving." It is therefore a demonic heresy to forbid marriage, "for everything God created is good, and nothing is to be rejected" (1 Tim. 4:3-4). In the well-known passage enjoining subjection to the Roman authorities, Paul writes, "There is no authority except that which God has established. The authorities that exist have been established by God. Consequently, he who rebels against authority is rebelling against *what God has instituted*" (Rom. 13:1-2). The final clause is a translation of *diatagē*, a Greek word for "commandment," which is effectively rendered as "ordinance" in the King James Version. The apostle Peter echoes Paul's teaching in even clearer words: "Submit yourselves for the Lord's sake to every *authority instituted* among men" (1 Pet. 2:13); the italicized words translate the Greek word *ktisis*, the regular biblical word for "creation" or "creature." It seems plain, therefore, that civil authority belongs to the created order; the state is founded in an ordinance of God.

These incidental biblical givens about the creational nature of marriage and the state do not prove that societal structures in general belong to creation; they merely illustrate a point that follows from the basic confession of the universal scope of God's ordinances. The same holds true for such structures as the family and the church and for such modern institutions as businesses and schools. They too are grounded in the realities of God's world order and are therefore not arbitrary in their configuration. All schools and businesses have certain constant features that distinguish them from other institutions. The constancy of those distinguishing features must be referred to the nature of reality as given by God. Educators, for example, develop an intuitive sense for the distinctive structure of a school; if school board members try to run it like a business, they recognize that violence is being done to the nature of an educational institution. They are attuned to its normative structure, to the law that holds for it. Similarly, business executives know that a business cannot be treated like a family. Relations in a firm have to be "businesslike" to be normative; they are judged by distinctive standards of propriety that are not arbitrary.

What is true for societal life is also true of culture. The worlds of art and pedagogy are bound to given standards. Much of modern art, with its refusal to recognize any aesthetic norms, edges toward nihilism: it manifests a glorification of autonomous human creativity, and in doing so denies God's creativity in the aesthetic realm. Not all art is good art. Both artists and aestheticians are called, each in their own ways, to discern the criteria that define good art—criteria that are not arbitrary but rooted in a given order of things that must be honored. Things are no different in the field of pedagogy and child rearing. There are stages of emotional and intellectual maturity in the child's development that must be respected by the educator. The teacher cannot afford to ignore a child's natural curiosity or spontaneous playfulness. A pedagogy that ignores these given realities is antinormative; it flies in the face of the law of creation.

And so we could go on. Human emotionality and sexuality, for example, are not normless. Our reasoning is subject to the laws of thought, our speech to semantic principles. Everything is subject to given laws of God: everything is creational. All the departments of what theologians have called "natural life" are part and parcel of creaturely reality. They are appointed and ordained by God as prov-inces of the earthly realm he created.

The Revelation of Creation

We have defined creation law as the totality of God's sovereign activity toward the created cosmos. Included in that sovereign ac-tivity is God's revelation in creation, what has traditionally been called "general revelation." The law of creation is *revelatory*: it im-parts knowledge. The Scriptures are quite explicit about this.

> The heavens declare the glory of God;
>   the skies proclaim the work of his hands.
> Day after day they pour forth speech;
>   night after night they display knowledge.
> There is no speech or language
>   where their voice is not heard.
> Their voice goes out into all the earth,
>   their words to the ends of the world.
>
> (Ps. 19:1-4)

In the New Testament it is especially Paul who stresses God's revelation in creation. At Lystra, where the pagans wanted to wor-ship Barnabas as Zeus, Paul rushed into the crowd of would-be worshipers and called on them to turn from their idols to "a living God who made the heaven and the earth and the sea and all that is in them." Of that Creator he went on to say, "Yet he has not left himself without testimony: He has shown kindness by giving you rain from heaven and crops in their seasons; he provides you with plenty of food and fills your hearts with joy" (Acts 14:17). Not long after that, in Corinth, Paul wrote his famous letter to the Christians in the Roman capital; in it he rehearses the same theme. He speaks of God's wrath for mankind, who by their wickedness suppress the truth. This charge is not unfair, "since what may be known about God is plain to them, because God has made it plain to them. For since the creation of the world God's invisible qualities—his eternal power and divine nature—have been clearly seen, being understood from what has been made, so that men are without excuse" (Rom. 1:18-20). This is very bold language. The truth is available to man-kind, but we repress it. We "clearly see" and "understand" God's eternal power and divine nature (synonyms, or near enough, for what we have been calling God's law and his sovereignty), but we twist and distort this knowledge. Moreover, this knowledge derives "from creation" (the Greek noun is *ktisis*, and the preposition normally means "from," not "since") and from "what has been made" (Greek *ta poiēmata*, "the works of the craftsman's art"). God speaks plainly through his works, but we perversely mishear him.

Nevertheless, in spite of human perversity, some of God's message in creation gets through. Even the Gentiles, "who do not have the law" (i.e., the Mosaic law, God's spelling out of his creational law for Old Testament Israel), have a sense of its normative demands, as Paul adds in the next chapter of his letter: "Indeed, when Gentiles, who do not have the law, do by nature things required by the law, they are a law for themselves, even though they do not have the law, since they show that the requirements of the law are written on their hearts, their consciences also bearing witness, and their thoughts now accusing, now even defending them" (Rom. 2:14-15). Even without God's explicit verbal positivization of the creational norms for justice and faithfulness, stewardship and respect, people have an intuitive sense of normative standards for conduct. One word for that intuitive attunement to creational normativity is *conscience*. As human beings we are so interwoven into the fabric of a normed creation that in spite of our religious mutiny we conform to creational standards "by nature," by virtue of our very constitution as creatures. Creational law speaks so loudly, impresses itself so forcefully on human beings, even in the delusions of paganism, that its normative demands are driven home into their inmost being, are "written on their hearts" like the indelible inscription of a law code on a clay tablet. This does not refer to some innate virtue of "natural man," unaffected by sin, but to the finger of the sovereign Creator engraving reminders of his norms upon human sensibilities even in the midst of apostasy. God does not leave himself unattested; he refuses to be ignored. He asserts himself in an unmistakable display of his "eternal power and divine nature" so that we cannot fail to take note of the Creator's claims on our obedience.

All of this probably is best illustrated in the Old Testament idea of "wisdom." For the wise man of the book of Proverbs, writes Old Testament scholar James Fleming, "wisdom . . . was wrought into

the constitution of the universe," so that "man's wisdom was to know this divine Wisdom—plan, order—and attune his ways to it." Consequently, "wisdom meant conforming to the divine constitution. One must find out what it is, then order himself accordingly." In a word, "wisdom is ethical conformity to God's creation."*
Thus there are two senses of wisdom, corresponding to law and subject in creation: on the law side is the divine wisdom, God's plan or order, "wrought into the constitution of the universe"; on the subject side is human wisdom, the attunement or conformity to the creational order.

It is as wisdom on the law side that we must understand the term appearing in the early chapters of the book of Proverbs. There Wisdom is personified as a woman standing in public places, where all can hear her, calling out to the heedless mass of men:

> How long will you simple ones love your simple ways?
>   How long will mockers delight in mockery
>   and fools hate knowledge?
> If you had responded to my rebuke,
>   I would have poured out my heart to you
>   and made my thought known to you.
>
>   (Prov. 1:22-23)

This call going out to all people is the appeal of creational normativity, God's knocking at the door of our hearts and minds, urging us to open and respond to the ways of his law. To those who give heed Wisdom promises the riches of her knowledge; those who ignore her are fools and scoffers.

The connection between Wisdom and creation is made very explicit in Proverbs 8. Again she cries out in public, "I raise my voice to all mankind" (Prov. 8:4). But she relates this to her role in creation:

> The Lord possessed me at the beginning of his work,
>   before his deeds of old;
> I was appointed from eternity,
>   from the beginning, before the world began. . . .
> I was there when he set the heavens in place,
>   when he marked out the horizon on the face of the deep,

---

*James Fleming, *Personalities of the Old Testament* (New York: Scribners, 1939), p. 502.

when he established the clouds above
    and fixed securely the fountains of the deep,
when he gave the sea its boundary
    so the waters would not overstep his command,
and when he marked out the foundations of the earth.
    Then I was the 'amōn at his side.

(Prov. 8:22-23, 27-30)

In a bold metaphor the poet has Wisdom describe herself as a kind of living blueprint, preceding creation but present at its execution. It seems to be the law of creation before creation, pictured as a personified "artist's conception" that accompanies him in his work. The last lines quoted stress that this work involves the imposition of limits on creation; in that activity of God, Wisdom is "beside him like an 'amōn." I will add my guess to those that have already been made ("darling and delight," "master workman," "little child") about the meaning of that obscure Hebrew word. I would suggest that it means something like a scale model, a fixed point of reference that serves the craftsman as a standard in building. As God the craftsman fashions the world, Wisdom is the standard by which he works.

It is this personified Wisdom, the prototype of the universe, of whom it is said in Proverbs 9 that she has built her house with seven pillars (probably another reference to creation) and prepares a feast in it to which all are invited: "Leave your simple ways and you will live; walk in the way of understanding" (Prov. 9:6). This invitation is contrasted with the siren song of Lady Folly (see Prov. 9:13-18) and forms a fitting introduction to "the proverbs of Solomon" that begin in the next chapter. Those proverbs represent the feast of insight and understanding to which Lady Wisdom invites mankind. They deal largely with the practical wisdom necessary for everyday life, born of a God-fearing sensitivity to the creation order in family life, farming, commerce, and administration. The wisdom of Proverbs is the fruit of God's revelation in creation.

The conception of wisdom as the normative creation order is not limited to the book of Proverbs, of course. The book of Job is filled with it (especially the famous passages in chapters 38-41), and so is Ecclesiastes. But what is perhaps the most instructive passage with respect to the revelation of God's wisdom in creation is not found in one of the "wisdom books" at all. I am referring to the end of chapter 28 in Isaiah:

> Listen and hear my voice;
>   pay attention and hear what I say.
> When a farmer plows for planting, does he
>   plow continually
> Does he keep on breaking up and harrowing the soil?
> When he has leveled the surface,
>   does he not sow caraway and scatter cummin?
> Does he not plant wheat in its place,
>   barley in its plot,
>   and spelt in its field?
> *His God instructs him*
>   *and teaches him the right way.*
>
> Caraway is not threshed with a sledge,
>   nor is a cartwheel rolled over cummin;
> caraway is beaten out with a rod,
>   and cummin with a stick.
> Grain must be ground to make bread;
>   so one does not go on threshing it forever.
> Though he drives the wheels of his threshing cart over it,
>   his horses do not grind it.
> *All this also comes from the Lord Almighty,*
>   *wonderful in counsel and magnificent in wisdom.*
>
>   (Isa. 28:23-29)

The Lord teaches the farmer his business. There is a right way to plow, to sow, and to thresh, depending on the kind of grain he is growing. Dill, cummin, wheat, and spelt must all be treated differently. A good farmer knows that, and this knowledge too is from the Lord, for the Lord teaches him. This is not a teaching through the revelation of Moses and the Prophets, but a teaching through the revelation of creation—the soil, the seeds, and the tools of his daily experience. It is by listening to the voice of God in the work of his hands that the farmer finds the way of agricultural wisdom.

An implication of the revelation of God in creation is that the creation order is *knowable*. That is also the significance of the *call* of Wisdom to all—she appeals to everyone to pay attention and learn from her, for insight and understanding are genuinely available to them if they heed her. This fundamental knowability of the creation order is the basis of all human understanding, both in science and in everyday life. Again, this is generally admitted readily enough in the case of the natural sciences (although even here the humanistic philosophy of science has long since abandoned the idea of a given order of nature that science can know), but it meets with skepticism and outright disbelief when it is applied to the social sciences and the humanities. The same applies to the everyday knowing that precedes science. If we suppose for the sake of argument that there really are given creational norms for aesthetic life, for example, can they ever be known, especially in this sinful dispensation? If there is a normative structure for the school, for the state, for the business enterprise, do we have any cognitive access to it? Don't the conflicting interpretations and theories of even like-minded people about these realities give the lie to their knowability? Doesn't the old adage of aesthetic relativism—*de gustibus non disputandum est*—apply across the board to all questions of "value"?

This is a point at which worldviews divide. Christians, too, differ on this fundamental point of the knowability of creational law. Many will argue either that the creational scheme of things has been altered by the fall (or at least so obscured as to be inaccessible to our knowing) or else that human powers of cognition have been so corrupted by sin as to make them unable to discern God's will for such areas as art, economics, or politics. Such views either fail to do justice to the constancy of God's will for creation (or to its revelatory power) or else they downplay the renewing power of Jesus Christ in restoring our faculty of discernment. We will deal with both of these errors in the chapters on sin and redemption. In the present context we shall restrict ourselves to bringing forward one more scriptural argument (in addition to those already adduced) in favor of the knowability of creational norms. It is what the Scriptures say about *spiritual discernment*.

From among a number of representative passages in the New Testament on this theme (e.g., Eph. 1:17-18, Rom. 12:2, Heb. 5:14) we may select the following words of Paul addressed to the Colossians: "We have not stopped praying for you and asking God *to fill you with the knowledge of his will through all spiritual wisdom and understanding*. And we pray this in order that you may live a life worthy of the Lord and may please him in every way" (Col. 1:9-10). There is a spiritual discernment necessary if we are to know God's

There are many things about which the Scriptures are silent, but about which we must nevertheless seek to know the Lord's will. Above and beyond the explicit guidance of Scripture we need "spiritual wisdom and understanding." Traditionally, Christians have understood this to refer to the guidance necessary when making such momentous personal decisions as the choice of a marriage partner, the selection of a vocation, the consideration of a move to another country, or the like—in short, to what we have called the particular aspects of God's law in our lives, his guidance or calling. This is undoubtedly part of what Paul has in mind here, but can we exclude the *general* aspects of God's law, the universal normative principles that govern cultural and societal pursuits such as journalism, education, advertising, international relations? In these areas, too, the Bible does not give more than general parameters. Must we not seek to know and honor the area-specific will of God there too? To ask the question is to answer it. The implicit division between private and public life that many Christians make in applying Paul's words is quite arbitrary. It is in fact based on an unwarranted dualism in their worldview.

The parallel with "guidance" and "calling" is also instructive in others ways. In the case of a specific decision, we confess that there is a will of God that we are called to know and that God promises to reveal to us. Through a well-informed assessment of the factors involved, through consultation with trusted Christian advisors, through prayer and searching the Scriptures, we seek God's will; through the gift of "spiritual wisdom and understanding" we begin to discern it. Sometimes we make our decision in full assurance of having found God's way, but more often we do so with some hesitancy, remaining open to correction. Either way we may be making a choice against the advice of fellow Christians whose wisdom and discernment we respect. But the point is that the lack of assurance or unanimity does not invalidate the basic Christian confession that there *is* a will of God for my life, that it *can* be known, and that I *must* seek it and act on it. Precisely the same considerations apply to the discernment of the general creational norms that hold for every area of human affairs. That, too, involves the perceptive experience and investigation of immediate reality, teamwork and sharing with brothers and sisters in the same field, earnest prayer for guidance and insight, constant reference to Scripture, and familiarity with its overarching themes. And here too a measure of "spiritual wisdom and understanding" is indispensable, for human life in all its aspects is a thoroughly spiritual affair. Christians of all vocations and walks of life—business executives, farmers, academics, politicians, educators, homemakers, lawyers—must take to heart, not only in their private but also in their professional capacity, the well-known exhortation of the apostle, "Do not conform any longer to the pattern of this world, but be transformed by the renewing of your mind. *Then you will be able to test and approve what God's will is—his good, pleasing and perfect will*" (Rom. 12:2). To sum up, the whole world of our experience is constituted by the creative will and wisdom of God, and that will and wisdom—that is, *his law*— is everywhere in principle knowable by virtue of God's creational revelation.

One final point requires attention before we leave the subject of creation and revelation: How does God's speech in creation relate to his speech in Scripture? In putting such a great emphasis on general revelation, are we not in danger of minimizing special revelation? Do we not thereby compromise the Reformation's great principle of *sola Scriptura*?

This is a legitimate concern. To clarify the issue, we should first of all note that biblical revelation includes a great deal that has no parallel whatever in creational revelation. In a fundamental sense the Scriptures are the story of our sin in Adam and God's forgiving grace in Christ. Creation, by contrast, does not tell a story at all, nor does it tell anything of that sin or grace. As a message of salvation its revelation is useless. In that regard the two revelations are not comparable. They *are* comparable, however, as manifestations of God's *law*, as two ways of making known his *will*, specifically for human life. It is only in that sense that the question of Scripture arises in the present context.

Again, the analogy with "guidance" can be helpful. It is certainly true that a preoccupation with "the leading of the Spirit" in determining God's will for the decisions of everyday life can result in an undervaluing of Scripture, but that is not at all a necessary consequence of an emphasis on seeking God's will in our daily lives. A sound approach to guidance will always stress the primacy and indispensability of Scripture as well as the exercise of "sanctified common sense," but it will not thereby downplay the reality of a knowable and specific will of God for our personal lives. In fact, the Scriptures themselves by their insistent teaching of God's lordship over *all* of our lives continually drive us to consider questions of guidance. Suppose John, a college senior, has to decide whether to go on to seminary or to pursue graduate studies in philosophy. Scripture does not decide that question for him. Instead it gives him certain indispensable guidelines: he must seek the Lord's will in all things, he must be a good steward of the gifts God gives him, he must do all to the glory of God, God has a plan for his life and has been guiding him since childhood, he must subordinate his own wishes and desires to God's, and so on. But these guidelines press him on to a consideration of what God's will is in this situation, what gifts he has to be a steward of, what is most glorifying to God in this particular case, what God's plan and guidance have been in his life to this point, what personal preferences must be downplayed, and so on. In considering all these individual questions he must continually check back with Scripture to make sure his bearings are right, but he would be foolish and irresponsible if he let a stray text decide the matter for him without considering available graduate schools, his own talents and temperament, specific historical needs, and so on.

The matter is no different in the case of Scripture and creational normativity in general. The Scriptures teach us to look for God's norms in our experience and also serve to greatly improve our vision. There are two images that can help us to understand the relationship of God's revelation in his Word and in his work. The first is John Calvin's image of the Scriptures as spectacles through which we are enabled to read the book of nature:

> Just as old or bleary-eyed men and those with weak vision, if you thrust before them a most beautiful volume, even if they recognize it to be some sort of writing, yet can scarcely construe two words, but with the aid of spectacles will begin to read distinctly; so Scripture, gathering up the otherwise confused knowledge of God in our minds, having dispersed our dullness, clearly shows us the true God.

> (*Inst.*, 1.6.1)

Another way of saying this is that we can discern creational normativity best in the light of Scripture.

The "light" of Scripture suggests another image, too. Scripture is like a miner's lamp, which lights up the world wherever we turn to look at it. Miners working in an unlighted underground mine shaft cannot do their work without the lamp fitted to their helmets; they are helpless without it and therefore must take great care to see that it functions properly. Yet their attention while they work is turned to the rockface, not to the lamp. The lamp serves to illuminate the environment in which they are called to work, to enable them to discern the nature of what lies before them: earth and rock, ore and gangue. The Scriptures are like that. "Thy word is a lamp to my feet and a light to my path" (Ps. 119:105). But the path must nevertheless be *found* in the specific experience of my life, whatever my "walk of life."

What makes the light of Scripture so helpful and indispensable is that it spells out in clear human language what God's law is. Even without Scripture we have some notion of the requirements of justice, but Moses and the prophets, Jesus and the apostles put it into clear, unmistakable imperatives. Every society has some idea of the integrity of the family, but the Bible lays it down in inescapable and unequivocal terms. Some inkling of the need for responsible use of our resources is found almost everywhere, but the Scriptures unambiguously articulate the basic principle of stewardship. Perhaps the Bible's central command that we love our neighbor is most alien to natural man, but even this is understood to some degree by the apostate human race living in God's creation. Yet only the message of the Scriptures can make clear to Adam's children the centrality and radical nature of that basic command.

God's revelation in creation is not *verbal*; its message does not come to us in human language. "They have no speech, there are no words," writes David of the heavens telling the glory of God (Ps. 19:3). Mankind has in large measure lost the capacity to interpret what the heavens are saying in their wordless message. The Scriptures, on the other hand, are couched in the words of ordinary human discourse. In traditional terminology, they are *revelatio verbalis*, "word revelation," as opposed to *revelatio naturalis*, "revelation of nature" (i.e., of creation). They are plain in a way that general revelation never is, have a "perspicuity" that is not found in the book of nature. In a way, therefore, the Scriptures are like a verbal commentary on the dimly perceived sign language of creation. Or, to change the image slightly, the revelation of God's will in creation is like a verbal explanation that an architect gives to an incompetent builder who has forgotten how to read the blueprint. Without the explanation the builder is at a loss, able to puzzle out in general terms what the blueprint indicates perhaps—how many rooms and stories the building is to have and the like—but in the dark about some of the most basic features of its style and design, or even whether it is to be a house or a factory or a barn. With the explanations everything becomes much clearer, and the builder can proceed confidently with the task.

Perhaps the blueprint image can also make another point clearer. Let us suppose the architect has tape-recorded the explanation. Unable to consult the architect directly on every small point, the builder would have to depend on both the recording and the blueprint for sufficient information to put up the house—the recording for general information, and the blueprint for all the specific measurements and sizes and many other details that would likely become clear only on careful study and through experience as the building progresses. It is in this same way that we must continue to try to discern, through empirical study and historical experience, what God's specific norms are for areas of human life that the Scriptures do not explicitly address—industrial relations, for example, or the mass media, or literary criticism.

To say this is not to downgrade the authority of Scripture. The recorded explanations are indispensable, not least as an invaluable corrective for those who have their own interpretations of the blueprint. In all disputes of interpretation, the architect's own explanations are clearly the final authority. The point is that the explanations cannot be fully understood without the blueprint to which they refer, just as the blueprint is in turn largely unintelligible without the explanations. But it is inconceivable that the blueprint should ever be invoked against the architect's own verbal explanations of it. That would be insufferable arrogance on the part of the builder.

One final point should be made about the revelation of God's law in Scripture and in creation. We noted earlier that the Mosaic law was the divinely accredited implementation of creational law for ancient Israel. This means that the law of Moses is fixed between two reference points: creational law and ancient Israel, the universal and enduring principles of creation and the historical situation of a particular people (Israel) in a particular place (Palestine) at a particular time (the centuries between Moses and Christ). Because of this double reference, the coming of Christ also involves a "fulfillment" of the law in a double sense. On the one hand, the law is fulfilled in that the shadow is replaced by the substance, and Jewish law is no longer binding for the people of God. On the other hand, the law is fulfilled in that Christ reaffirms its deepest meaning (see Matt. 5:17). In other words, insofar as the Mosaic law is addressed to a particular phase of the history of God's people it has lost its validity, but insofar as it points to the enduring normativity of God's creation order it retains its validity. For example, the legislation concerning the year of Jubilee, applying as it does to an agrarian society in the ancient Near East, is no longer binding for the New Testament people of God, but in its reflection of a general principle of stewardship as a creational norm it should continue to function as a guide for the new Israel. The provision for a bill of divorce is no longer in effect, but it still stands as God's own reminder to us of a basic principle of justice: there must be legal guarantees to minimize the effects of the hardness of the human heart. The same could be said concerning the laws for tithing, protection of the poor and sojourners, and so on.

Another way of saying this is that God did the implementing for his people in the Old Testament, while in the New he in large measure gives us the freedom in Christ to do our own implementing. That is the point of Paul's letter to the Galatians. But in both cases he holds us to the blueprint of the law of creation. In the Old Testament the explanations he gave included detailed instructions for the implementation of the blueprint; that was by way of apprenticeship. In Christ we are journeyman builders—still bound to the architect's explicit directions, but with considerable freedom of implementation as new situations arise.

The Development of Creation

In our earlier discussion of the creation account in Genesis 1, we pointed out that the six days of creation actually represent a finishing and a furnishing of an originally unfinished and empty "earth." There is a process of development and evolution as the earthly realm assumes, step by step, the contours of the variegated world of our experience. On the sixth day this process is completed with the creation of man, and on the seventh day God rests from his labors. This is not the end of the development of creation, however. Although God has withdrawn from the work of creation, he has put an image of himself on the earth with a mandate to continue. The earth had been completely unformed and empty; in the six-day process of development God had formed it and filled it—but not completely. People must now carry on the work of development: by being fruitful they must fill it even more; by subduing it they must form it even more. Mankind, as God's representatives on earth, carry on where God left off. But this is now to be a *human* development of the earth. The human race will fill the earth with its own kind, and it will form the earth for its own kind. From now on the development of the created earth will be *societal* and *cultural* in nature. In a single word, the task ahead is *civilization*.

Parallel with the distinction between the initial six days of world development and the subsequent task of human civilization is the distinction we made earlier between the direct and the indirect way God has of imposing his law on the cosmos. As we have noted, God's rule of law is immediate in nature, but mediate in culture and society. That distinction takes on a new significance at this point in the discussion. The *laws of nature* govern the earth as developed by God directly, in the so-called *creatio secunda*; the *norms* govern the earth as developed by God indirectly, through people, in what we might call the *creatio tertia*. Just as the eight creational "Let there be's" represent creational law as it holds for animal, vegetable, and mineral, so the fourfold "cultural mandate" represents creational law as it holds for society and culture.

That mandate, more properly called the "creation mandate," is of such foundational importance for the whole scriptural history of revelation, and therefore for a biblical worldview, that we would do well to look more closely at its wording:

> Be fruitful and increase in number; fill the earth and subdue it; rule over the fish of the sea, and the birds of the air and over every living creature that moves on the ground. (Gen. 1:28)

We should observe that the word *earth* occurs in the double sense we noted earlier. To subdue the earth (in the broad sense) involves having dominion over the populations of sea, air, and earth (in the narrow sense). The earth that people are to subdue is that whole earthly realm in need of forming and filling. It was formed by the divisions into sea, air, and earth, and these divisions were filled by fish, birds, and land animals, respectively. That is often how the Bible talks about the created cosmos: "For in six days the Lord made the heavens and the earth, the sea, and all that is in them" (Ex. 20:11; cf. Ps. 24:2 and Acts 14:15). The point is that only people are called to fill and form the whole earth; only of people can it be said "You made him ruler over the works of your hands; you put everything under his feet" (Ps. 8:6).

The creation mandate provides a sort of climax to the six days of creation. The stage with all its rich variety of props has been set by the stage director, the actors are introduced, and as the curtain rises and the stage director moves backstage, they are given their opening cue. The drama of human history is about to begin, and the first and foundational Word of God to his children is the command to "fill and subdue."

The drama itself begins in Genesis 2, opening with the words, "These are the generations of the heavens and the earth when they were created" (KJV). This is the first of ten sections in Genesis introduced by the phrase "these are the generations of . . ." in which the term generations (Hebrew tōledōt, literally "begettings") seems to mean something like "historical developments arising out of . . . ." History is the generational unfolding and opening up of the possibilities hidden in the womb of creation, both natural and human. Prototypical of this history is the misnamed "second account of creation" in Genesis 2, in which first Adam is "begotten" from the earth and later Eve from Adam, and man is placed in the garden to "fill it and keep it" (Gen. 2:15, KJV). These are the paradigmatic beginnings of man's filling and subduing the earth. Adam and Eve, as the first married couple, represent the beginnings of societal life; their task of tending the garden, the primary task of agriculture, represents the beginnings of cultural life. The mandate to develop creation is being fulfilled in history.

All of this has the most direct and immediate bearing on a biblical worldview and its conception of creation. Creation is not something that, once made, remains a static quantity. There is, as it were, a growing up (though not in a biological sense), an unfolding of creation. This takes place through the task that people have been given of bringing to fruition the possibilities of development implicit in the work of God's hands. The given reality of the created order is such that it is *possible* to have schools and industry, printing and rocketry, needlepoint and chess. The creational law is crying out to be positivized in new and amazing ways. The whole vast range of human civilization is neither the spectacle of the arbitrary aberrations of an evolutionary freak nor the inspiring panorama of the creative achievements of the autonomous Self; it is rather a display of the marvelous wisdom of God in creation and the profound meaningfulness of our task in the world. We are called to participate in the ongoing creational work of God, to be God's helper in executing to the end the blueprint for his masterpiece.

The meaning of history, therefore, must be sought against the background of the human management of God's work. There are stages of development in creation corresponding to the stages of human civilization. What is involved here is the opening up of creation through the historical process. If we fail to see this, if we conceive of the historical differentiation that has led to such institutions as the school and the business enterprise, and such developments as urbanization and the mass media, as being basically outside the scope of creational reality and its responsible management by the human race, we will be tempted to look upon these and similar matters as fundamentally alien to God's purposes in the world and will tend to brand them as being inherently "secular," either in a religiously neutral or an outright negative sense. Our approach to history will be fundamentally reactionary, though we may make our peace, willy- nilly, with the present stage of historical development in the postindustrial West.

However, if we see that human history and the unfolding of culture and society are integral to creation and its development, that they are not outside God's plans for the cosmos, despite the sinful aberrations, but rather were built in from the beginning, were part of the blueprint that we never understood before, then we will be much more open to the positive possibilities for service to God in such areas as politics and the film arts, computer technology and business administration, developmental economics and skydiving. This does not entail a naive and starry-eyed acceptance of modern scientism, technocracy, and capitalism—the civilization of the West is admittedly in the grip of a disastrous process of secularization, after all—but it does entail a resolute refusal to abandon our civilization to that process or to concede the point that God's creative hand in absent in the culture-building of Faustian man. If God does not give up on the works of his hands, we may not either.

A discussion of creation in terms of Genesis 1 and 2 (the development of the earth) can easily give the impression of a cultural optimism, since we have not yet talked of Genesis 3 (the fall and the curse, as well as the promise). There is always something abstract and unreal about talking about creation apart from sin and redemption. It may be helpful, therefore, to illustrate the point about the development of creation with an analogy that anticipates the points we will consider in the next two chapters.

Earthly creation preceding the events recorded in Genesis 3 is like a healthy newborn child. In every respect it can be pronounced "very good," but this does not mean that change is not required. There is something seriously wrong if the baby remains in its infancy: it is meant to grow, develop, mature into adulthood. Suppose now that while the child is still an infant it contracts a serious chronic disease for which there is no known cure, and that it grows up an invalid, the disease wasting its body away. It is clear that there are two clearly distinguishable processes going on in its body as it approaches adolescence: one is the process of maturation and growth, which continues in spite of the sickness and which is natural, normal, and good; the other is the progress of the disease, which distorts and impairs the healthy functioning of the body. Now suppose further that the child has reached adolescence when a cure is found for the sickness, and it slowly begins to recover its health. As the child approaches adulthood there is now a third process at work in its body: the process of healing, which counteracts and nullifies the action of the disease and which has no other purpose than to bring the youth to healthy adulthood, in which only the normal processes of a sound body will take place. The child will then be said to be restored to health after these many years.

There are weaknesses to every analogy, and the most glaring in this one is that the process of creational unfolding in history is not like a process of biological growth but rather like a process of responsible development. Nevertheless, it can serve to make a significant point: the ravages of sin do not annihilate the normative creational development of civilization, but rather are parasitical upon it. Maturation and deterioration can be so intimately inter-twined in reality that only scripturally directed sensitivity to the creational norm (some idea of what a healthy body is like) can hope to discern the difference. Yet it is an absolutely fundamental dis-tinction, and one neglects it only at the peril of falling into either cultural pessimism (which sees only the debilitating effects of the sin) or cultural optimism (which sees only the normative develop-ment of creational possibilities).

Adam and Eve in Paradise had not yet reached the level of development that God had planned for them. Theologians have on the whole granted this to be true (they have typically postulated a progression from Adam's state to the state of glory in God's plan for human development), and yet they often overlook its broader im-plications for creation and history.

The same can be said for eschatology in general. Foundational to everything we have been saying is the conviction, based on the Bible's testimony, that the Lord does not forsake the work of his hands. In faithfulness he upholds his creation order. Even the great crisis that will come on the world at Christ's return will not anni-hilate God's creation or our cultural development of it. The new heaven and the new earth the Lord has promised will be a contin-uation, purified by fire, of the creation we now know. There is no reason to believe that the cultural dimensions of earthly reality (except insofar as they are involved in sin) will be absent from the new, glorified earth that is promised. In fact, the biblical indications point in the opposite direction. Describing the new earth as the new Jerusalem, John writes that "the kings of the earth will bring their splendor into it. . . . The glory and the honor of the nations will be brought into it" (Rev. 21:24, 26). This very likely refers to the cultural treasures of mankind will be purified by passing through the fires of judgment, like gold in a crucible.

A passage that is sometimes adduced against this view is 2 Peter 3:10, but in fact this passage lends support to it. In the RSV it reads, "But the day of the Lord will come like a thief, and then the heavens will pass away with a loud noise, and the elements will be dissolved with fire, and the earth and the works that are upon it will be burned up." However, all but one of the oldest and most reliable Greek manuscripts do not have the final words "will be burned up" but instead have "will be found," which makes quite a difference. (This is the Greek text accepted by the more recent translations, such as the JB and NIV, which read, somewhat obscurely, "will be laid bare.") The text therefore teaches that in spite of the passing away of the heavens and the dissolving of the elements, "the earth and the works that are upon it" will survive. And as for the passing away and the dissolving, this certainly does not refer to annihilation or complete destruction. A few verses earlier Peter had written that the world "was destroyed" in former times (v. 6), referring to the catastrophic destruction wreaked by the Flood, and he is drawing a parallel between that judgment and the one to come. The day of the Lord will bring the fires of judgment and a cataclysmic convulsion of all creation, but what emerges from the crucible will be "a new heaven and a new earth, the home of righteousness" (v. 13), and it is presumably there that "the earth and the works that are upon it will be found," now purified from the filth and perversion of sin.

In light of what we have been saying about the earthly creation and man's task of subduing and developing it, those purified works on the earth must surely include the products of human culture. There is no reason to doubt that they will be transfigured and transformed by their liberation from the curse, but they will be in essential continuity with our experience now—just as our resurrected bodies, though glorified, will still be bodies. It may be, as Herman Bavinck has suggested, that human life on the new earth, compared to that life now, will be like the colorful butterfly that develops our of the pupa: dramatically different, but the same creature. Perhaps the most fitting symbol of the development of creation from the primordial past to the eschatological future is the fact that the Bible begins with a garden and ends with a city—a city filled with "the glory and the honor of the nations."

The Goodness of Creation

Before turning to the theme of human sin and the devastation it works, we must emphasize a fundamental point that we have been assuming in our discussion of creation thus far: the crucial biblical teaching that creation before and apart from sin is wholly and unambiguously *good*.

On seven different occasions in the Genesis 1 account of creation, God pronounces his works of creation to be good, climaxing in the last verse with the words "And God saw everything that he had make, and behold, it was very good." God does not make junk, and we dishonor the Creator if we take a negative view of the work of his hands when he himself takes such a positive view. In fact, so positive a view did he take of what he had created that he refused to scrap it when mankind spoiled it, but determined instead, at the cost of his Son's life, to make it new and good again. God does not make junk, and he does not junk what he has made.

In the early church there was a heresy called Gnosticism that denied the goodness of creation in a fundamental way. It held that the Creator of Genesis 1 was a subordinate evil deity who had rebelled against the supreme good God, and that the world he made was an evil place, a prison from which people had to be rescued. The Gnostics considered salvation to be a flight away from this evil world in withdrawal and detachment in order to achieve a kind of mystical union with the supreme God. Gnosticism posed a significant threat to the early church and was fiercely attacked by such Church Fathers as Irenaeus. Already in the days of the apostles the danger of such a heresy was apparent. This is what Paul seems to have had in mind when he wrote to Timothy about a special message from the Spirit in regard to a demonic teaching that would appear "in the last days" prohibiting marriage and the eating of certain kinds of foods. Such a message, warns Paul, depreciates God's good gifts, "which God created to be received with thanksgiving by those who believe and know the truth." He then adds the following ringing manifesto: "For everything created by God is good, and nothing is to be rejected if it is received with thanksgiving; for then it is consecrated [or: sanctified] by the word of God and prayer" (1 Tim. 4:4-5, RSV). If Timothy will drive home *this* point to the believers, says Paul, then he will be "a good minister of Christ Jesus" (v. 6). Against the Gnostic maligning of God's creation (or some part of it) he must proclaim the goodness of all creation.

The ramifications of this basic confession are far-reaching, especially if we recognize that creation includes everything wrought by God's wisdom (including such institutions as marriage). It is the biblical antidote to all worldviews, religions, and philosophies that single out some feature or features of the created order as the cause of the human predicament, whether that be the body, temporality, finitude, emotionality, authority, rationality, individuality, technology, culture, or what have you. All of these have been scapegoats that have drawn attention away from the real root of the trouble, human religious mutiny against the Creator and his laws for the world—a mutiny that most assuredly is *not* part of God's creation and its goodness. Deeply ingrained in the children of Adam is the tendency to blame some aspect of creation (and by implication the Creator) rather than their own rebellion for the misery of their condition.

The goodness of creation also underscores another point we have been assuming all along—namely, that subjection to law is not a restriction upon God's creatures, particularly men and women, but rather that it makes possible their free and healthy functioning. If creation is fundamentally constituted by law, is in fact defined by the law-subject correlation, then law cannot be a primarily negative category. To the religion of the Renaissance humanism that has shaped the secularism of the West, this is blasphemy. Humanism defines humans in terms of freedom, and defines freedom as autonomy, obeying no law but one's own. Biblical religion contends that the very opposite is true: people are defined by their servanthood, and servanthood is defined by heteronomy, obeying the law of the Creator. Humanism considers law to be the *contradiction* of freedom; the Bible considers law to be *condition* of freedom.

"Law" here means in the first place creational law, the order of God's wisdom in all the world. But it also includes "positive law"—the way in which creational norms are positivized in specific ways in the state and the church, family and marriage, art and industry. Law is the condition for freedom and health in both senses, although positive law, as a human work, is often sinful and repressive. The abuse of positive law (essentially the abuse of authority) does not, however, negate the fundamental goodness of positive law itself (nor of authority).

The most striking illustration of the goodness of positive law can be found in the Mosaic law. As we have indicated earlier, this is God's own positivization of creational norms for ancient Israel. The books of the Old Testament never tire of praising its goodness and of stressing that safety and *shalom* can only be found by a return to the Torah. The longest psalm, Psalm 119, is one long paean of praise for the law of God in this sense.

3

Fall

We concluded our earlier discussion of worldview by underlining the centrality of creation, fall, and redemption in a reformational worldview. Having dealt briefly with the scope and some of the salient features of the idea of creation, we can now consider man's fall into sin and its consequences for the creation, the dwelling God originally made to be very good.

The Scope of the Fall

First of all, we must stress that the Bible teaches plainly that Adam and Eve's fall into sin was not just an isolated act of disobedience but an event of catastrophic significance for creation as a whole. Not only the whole human race but the whole nonhuman world too was caught up in the train of Adam's failure to heed God's explicit commandment and warning. The effects of sin touch all of creation; no created thing is in principle untouched by the corrosive effects of the fall. Whether we look at societal structures such as the state or family, or cultural pursuits such as art or technology, or bodily functions such as sexuality or eating, or anything at all within the wide scope of creation, we discover that the good handiwork of God has been drawn into the sphere of human mutiny against God. "The whole creation," Paul writes in a profound passage of Romans, "has been groaning as in the pains of childbirth right up to the present time" (Rom. 8:22).

We should note at this point that we are using the word *creation* here (in line with Paul's usage in the quotation) to refer specifically to *earthly* creation, not to *heavenly* creation. Scripture does refer to

44

a mutiny in heaven among the angels, but it does not say that heaven was infected and enslaved as a result. Bondage does however characterize the *earthly* realm of God's dominions, the ordinary sphere of human life and experience. It is creation in this earthly sense that is tainted by sin throughout.

It is not difficult to find examples of the widespread effects of the fall in our world. Society is replete with such examples. The creational institution of marriage is under special attack in the contemporary West—divorce and serial monogamy are examples of the perversion and violation of God's good design for creaturely life. The family is severely strained by the disruptive forces of a materialistic society in which parents often neglect the interests of their children for the sake of their careers. The state as an ordinance of God is twisted and distorted in the various kinds of totalitarianism and tyranny in the world today. Distortion is also evident in political systems that encourage the formation of government policy simply in response to the pressure of special interest groups rather than in response to the demand for true justice for all. We see the exploitation of creational structures in the industrial warfare so prevalent in many Western economies, and likewise in the waste of environmental resources. Disregard for social consequences as well as naked greed corrupt the good creational make-up of labor unions and corporations alike, both of which should be governed by considerations of stewardship.

Our cultural life also provides many examples of the perversion of God's good creation. Think of kitsch in the arts, or bad taste in general, in painting, music, poetry. Consider within the academic realm the widespread phenomenon of scientism, of sloppy methodology and fallacious reasoning. Observe how efficiency has become the overriding concern in the world of technology, and note the exaggerated attachment to technique in human affairs. Everywhere we turn, the good possibilities of God's creation are misused, warped, and exploited for sinful ends.

Distortion is perhaps most obvious in our personal lives, where the effects of the fall are most readily recognized by Christians. Murder, adultery, theft, blasphemy, and many other vices are obvious and widespread infringements on God's creational design for human life. Perhaps less obvious are such violations as emotional disturbances and mental diseases; these too are distortions of creaturely human functions and participate in the groaning of creation. The Bible even ties bodily sickness, the causes of which so often lie outside the sphere or our personal responsibility, to the root cause of human sinfulness (see, for example, 1 Cor. 11:30).

Everyone senses intuitively that in all the above-mentioned areas we must distinguish between what is "normal" and what is "abnormal." Although we may find it difficult to formulate criteria for defining normality, we are forced to use words that designate deviations from what we consider normal, whether they be ordinary words such as *abnormal*, *sick*, or *unhealthy*, or more scientific terms such as *dysfunctional*, *maladjusted*, or *pathological*. The Bible too acknowledges this reality, using such strong terms as *corruption*, *vanity*, and *bondage*. This language points to a central scriptural teaching— namely, that wherever anything wrong exists in the world, anything we experience as antinormative, evil, distorted, or sick, there we meet the perversion of God's good creation.

It is one of the unique and distinctive features of the Bible's teaching on the human situation that all evil and perversity in the world is ultimately the result of humanity's fall, of its refusal to live according to the good ordinances of God's creation. Human disobedience and guilt lie in the last analysis at the root of all the troubles on earth. That the fall is at the root of evil is most clear for specifically human evil as it is manifested, for example, in personal, cultural, and societal distortions. Since all have fallen in Adam, evil in human life in general originates in enmity toward God.

But the effects of sin range more widely than the arena of specifically human affairs, touching also the nonhuman world. Two biblical passages in particular make this wider scope of sin unmistakable. The first is Genesis 3:17, in which immediately after the fall God says to Adam, "Cursed is the ground because of you." The very soil is affected by Adam's sin, making agriculture more difficult. A more extensive passage is the one in Romans to which we have already alluded. The passage as a whole reads as follows:

> The creation waits in eager expectation for the sons of God to be revealed. For the creation was subjected to frustration, not by its own choice, but by the will of the one who subjected it, in hope that the creation itself will be liberated from its bondage to decay and brought into the glorious freedom of the children

of God. We know that the whole creation has been groaning as in the pains of childbirth right up to the present time. (Rom. 8:19-22)

Paul states that the whole creation, not just the human world, was subjected to frustration (i.e., to "vanity" or "futility" or "pointlessness") by the will of "the one who subjected it" (i.e., Adam, through his disobedience). That vanity seems to be the same as the "bondage to decay" from which creation will be liberated. Thus, we learn from Paul that the creation in its entirety is ensnared in the throes of antinormativity and distortion, though it will one day be liberated.

All of creation participates in the drama of man's fall and ultimate liberation in Christ. Though the implications are not easy to understand, this principle is a clear scriptural teaching. We will see it emphasized again when we come to speak of the kingdom of God as the restoration of creation. At bottom, it seems, all kinds of evil—whether sickness or death or immorality or maladjustments—are related in the Scriptures to human guilt.

The Relation of Sin and Creation

If it is true that Adam's sin carries in its train the corruption, at least in principle, of the whole of creation, then it becomes very important to understand how this corruption is related to the originally good creation. This relation is crucial for a Christian worldview. The central point to make is that, biblically speaking, sin neither abolishes nor becomes identified with creation. Creation and sin remain distinct, however closely they may be intertwined in our experience. Prostitution does not eliminate the goodness of human sexuality; political tyranny cannot wipe out the divinely ordained character of the state; the anarchy and subjectivism of much of modern art cannot obliterate the creational legitimacy of art itself. In short, evil does not have the power of bringing to naught God's steadfast faithfulness to the works of his hands.

Sin introduces an entirely new dimension to the created order. There is no sense in which sin "fits" in God's good handiwork. Rather, it establishes an unprecedented axis, as it were, along which it is possible to plot varying degrees of good and evil. Though fun-

damentally distinct from the good creation, this axis attaches itself
to creation like a parasite. Hatred, for example, has no place within
God's good creation. It is unimaginable in the context of God's plan
for the earth. Nevertheless, hatred cannot exist without the creational substratum of human emotion and healthy assertiveness.
Hatred participates simultaneously in the goodness of creation (man's
psychic makeup as part of his full humanity) and in the demonic
distortion of that good creation into something horrible and evil.
In sum, though evil exists only as a distortion of the good, it is
never reducible to the good.

Perhaps the point can be made plain by speaking here of two
"orders" that are irreducible to one another. In the words of John
Calvin, we must distinguish between "the order of creation" and
"the order of sin and redemption," which relate to each other as
health relates to sickness-and-healing. These two orders are in no
sense congruent with each other. At every point, so to speak, they
stand at right angles to each other, like the length and width of a
plane figure. The perversion of creation must never be understood
as a subdistinction within the order of creation, nor must creation
ever be explained as a function of perversion and redemption. As
fundamental orders of all reality they coexist—one original, the
other adventitious; one representing goodness, the other involving
deformity.

Or, to clarify the point further, we may say that sin and evil
always have the character of a caricature—that is, of a distorted
image that nevertheless embodies certain recognizable features. A
human being after the fall, though a travesty of humanity, is still
a human being, not an animal. A humanistic school is still a school.
A broken relationship is still a relationship. Muddled thinking is
still thinking. In each case, what something in fallen creation "still
is" points to the enduring goodness of creation—that is to say, to
the faithfulness of God in upholding the created order despite the
ravages of sin. Creation will not be suppressed in any final sense.

In the present context we must stress again that these two orders
are in no sense on a par with each other. Sin, an alien invasion of
creation, is completely foreign to God's purposes for his creatures.
It was not meant to be; it simply does not belong. Any theory that
somehow sanctions the existence of evil in God's good creation fails
to do justice to sin's fundamentally outrageous and blasphemous

character, and in some subtle or sophisticated sense lays the blame for sin on the Creator rather than on ourselves in Adam.

Structure and Direction

Perhaps it will be useful to reinforce the point by reintroducing two technical terms mentioned briefly earlier, terms that will play a key role in the rest of our discussion: *structure* and *direction*. In the context of the two "orders" of which we have been speaking, it can be said that structure refers to the order of creation, to the constant creational constitution of any thing, what makes it the thing or entity that it is. Structure is anchored in the law of creation, the creational decree of God that constitutes the nature of different kinds of creatures. It designates a reality that the philosophical tradition of the West has often referred to by such words as *substance*, *essence*, and *nature*.

Direction, by contrast, designates the order of sin and redemption, the distortion or perversion of creation through the fall on the one hand and the redemption and restoration of creation in Christ on the other. Anything in creation can be directed either toward or away from God—that is, directed either in obedience or disobedience to his law. This double direction applies not only to individual human beings but also to such cultural phenomena as technology, art, and scholarship, to such societal institutions as labor unions, schools, and corporations, and to such human functions as emotionality, sexuality, and rationality. To the degree that these realities fail to live up to God's creational design for them, they are misdirected, abnormal, distorted. To the degree that they still conform to God's design, they are in the grip of a countervailing force that curbs or counteracts the distortion. Direction therefore always involves two tendencies moving either for or against God.

We will see in the next chapter how redemption in Jesus Christ is the ultimate and decisive antidote to creational distortion and how it renews the possibility for true obedience. Outside of redemption, however, the devastating effects of sin in creation are also restrained and counteracted. God does not allow man's disobedience to turn his creation into utter chaos. Instead, he *maintains* his creation in the face of all the forces of destruction. Creation is like a leash that keeps a vicious dog in check. If it were not for the leash, the dog (fallen mankind) would go completely wild, causing incalculable harm and probably bringing destruction upon its own head. Redemption in this image is the uncanny power by which the dog's master persuades it to become friendly and cooperative, so that the dog no longer strains at the leash but seeks guidance from it. It is because of the leash that fallen man is still man, that crooked business is still business, that atheistic culture is still culture, and that humanistic insights are still genuine insights. The *structure* of all the creational givens persists despite their directional perversion. That structure, anchored in God's faithfulness, sets a limit on the corruption and bondage wrought by evil.

The theological tradition offers another way of understanding the restraint of creation. Some theologians have called the curbing of sin and its effects God's "common grace." Through God's goodness to all men and women, believers and unbelievers alike, God's faithfulness to creation still bears fruit in humankind's personal, societal, and cultural lives. "Common grace" is thus distinguished from God's "special grace" to his people, whereby sin is not only curbed but forgiven and atoned for, making possible true and genuine renewal from within. These terms can be improved upon perhaps (some have suggested that the term "conserving grace" is preferable to "common grace," since God's grace in Christ is also "common" in that it is offered to all humans), but they are valuable in that they reflect a recognition that God never lets go of his creatures, even in the face of apostasy, unbelief, and perversion. In our terminology, structure is never entirely obliterated by (mis)direction.

Again, we must point out that however intimately they may be intertwined in our actual experience, the strict distinction of structure and direction is of the greatest importance for a biblical worldview. The great danger is always to single out some aspect or phenomenon of God's good creation and identify it, rather than the alien intrusion of human apostasy, as the villain in the drama of human life. Such an error is tantamount to reducing direction to structure, to conceiving of the good-evil dichotomy as intrinsic to the creation itself. The result is that something in the good creation is declared evil. We might call this tendency "Gnosticism," as we discussed it in the preceding chapter. In the course of history, this "something" has been variously identified as marriage and certain kinds of foods (the Gnostic heresy Paul warns Timothy against in

1 Timothy 4), the body and its passions (Plato and much of Greek philosophy), culture in distinction from nature (Rousseau and much of Romanticism), institutional authority, especially in the state and the family (philosophical anarchism and much of depth psychology), technology and management techniques (Heidegger and Ellul, among others), or any number of things. There seems to be an ingrained Gnostic streak in human thinking, a streak that causes people to blame some aspect of God's handiwork for the ills and woes of the world we live in.

It is difficult to overemphasize the radical nature or the importance of the biblical condemnation of the Gnostic tendency. As far as I can tell, the Bible is unique in its uncompromising rejection of all attempts to confuse structure and direction or to identify part of creation as either the villain or the savior. All other religions, philosophies, and worldviews in one way or another fall into the trap of failing to keep creation and fall distinct, and this trap continues to be an ever-present danger for Christian thinking. We will have occasion to return to this point again and again.

The first three chapters of Genesis are crucial in this regard. Genesis 1 and 2 speak of the good creation and mankind's task within it; Genesis 3 tells the story of the fall and its consequences. The importance of this sequence lies in the fact that there is no corruption of the earth before the fall—an unstained creation *is* possible. The good creation precedes, and is therefore distinct from, the fall and its effects. Evil cannot be blamed on the good creation, but only on the fall. To take the modern liberal view (shared by virtually everyone but conservative evangelicals) that these chapters tell a myth about the human condition in which good and evil necessarily coexist is not only to rob them of their radical message but to contradict the very point they make. Evil is *not* inherent in the human condition: there once was a completely good creation and there will be again; hence, the restoration of creation is not impossible. Nothing in the world ought to be despaired of. Hope is grounded in the constant availability and the insistent presence of the good creation, even in those situations in which it is being terribly violated.

In the preceding chapter we saw that the law of creation manifests itself in another way since the intrusion of sin. Curbing sin and the evils that sin spawns, it prevents the complete disintegration of the earthly realm that is our home. The law, in other words, *impinges upon* its creaturely subjects. The law is "valid" in the sense that it holds, it is in force, it has come into effect. Ignoring the law of creation is impossible. The law is like a spring that can be pressed down or pushed out of sight only with great effort and that continues to make its presence felt even when repressed for a long time. The "structure" of a thing is the law that is in force for it, and no amount of repression or perversion will ever succeed in nullifying its presence and effect. The call for justice is present in the midst of tyranny. The creational appeal for commitment and love in human sexuality can be ignored only by actively turning a deaf ear to it—but that appeal will never be silent. Man's inhumanity to man always involves a more or less conscious ignoring of his humanity—and "ignoring" always implies an active disregard of a perceived claim to our awareness. Proverbs illustrates this forcefully: "In the heights, streets, and gates of the cities wisdom calls out: 'you who are simple, gain prudence; you who are foolish, gain understanding. Listen, for I have worthy things to say; I open my lips to speak what is right' " (Prov. 8:5, 6). God presses his claim upon us in the structure of his creation, regardless of our direction.

"World" as Perverted Creation

In our discussion of the fall we have stressed that nothing in creation lies outside its scope. As dirty water contaminates a clean pond, so the poisonous effects of the fall have fouled every aspect of creation. The term *world* in the Scriptures refers precisely to this wide scope of sin. A Christian's understanding of this word functions like a litmus test of his or her worldview.

World is used in a number of different ways in the Bible. Sometimes it means simply "creation," as in the expression "from the foundation of the world." Sometimes it means "the inhabited earth," as when Paul writes "Your faith is being reported all over the world" (Rom. 1:8). Other times, however, when representing something that pollutes and that Christians must avoid, *world* has a distinctly negative connotation. Consider the following phrases from Scripture:

Christus: "My kingdom is not of the *world*." (John 18:36)

Paul: "Do not conform any longer to the pattern of this *world*." (Rom. 12:2)

Paul: ". . . deceptive philosophy, which depends on human tradition and the basic principles of this *world* rather than on Christ." (Col. 2:8)

James: "Religion . . . is this: . . . to keep oneself from being polluted by the *world*." (James 1:27)

Peter: "If they have escaped the corruption of the *world* by knowing our Lord and Savior Jesus Christ . . ." (2 Pet. 2:20)

What precisely is meant by *world* (usually *kosmos* in Greek, sometimes *aiōn*) in this very negative sense? According to Herman Ridderbos, in Paul's usage it refers to "the totality of unredeemed life dominated by sin outside of Christ."* In other words, *world* designates the totality of sin-infected creation. Wherever human sinfulness bends or twists or distorts God's good creation, there we find the "world." *World* here is the rottenness of the earth, the antithesis of creational goodness. In a similar vein, James states bluntly, "Don't you know that friendship with the world is hatred toward God?" (James 4:4).

All of this may seem straightforward enough. We should note, however, that Christians of virtually every persuasion have tended to understand "world" to refer to a delimited area of the created order, an area that is usually called "worldly" or "secular" (from *saeculum*, the Latin rendering of *aiōn*), which includes such fields as art, politics, scholarship (excluding theology), journalism, sports, business, and so on. In fact, to this way of thinking, the "world" includes everything outside the realm of the "sacred," which consists basically of the church, personal piety, and "sacred theology." Creation is therefore divided up neatly (although the dividing line may

---

*Ridderbos, *Paul: An Outline of His Theology* (Grand Rapids: William B. Eerdmans, 1975), p. 91.

be defined differently by different Christians) into two realms: the secular and the sacred.

This compartmentalization is a very great error. It implies that there is no "worldliness" in the church, for example, and that no holiness is possible in politics, say, or journalism. It defines what is secular not by its religious orientation or direction (obedience or disobedience to God's ordinances) but by the creational neighborhood it occupies. Once again, it falls prey to that deep-rooted Gnostic tendency to depreciate one realm of creation (virtually all of society and culture) with respect to another, to dismiss the former as inherently inferior to the latter.

This tendency is a serious matter and has far-reaching consequences. Consider how it affects our reading of Scripture. When we read Christ's words "my kingdom is not of this world," many of us are inclined to understand it as an argument against Christian involvement in politics, for example. Instead, Jesus was saying that his kingship does not arise out of (Greek: *ek*) the perverted earth but derives from heaven. When James says that pure religion is to keep oneself unspotted from the world, we too easily read this as a warning against dancing or card playing or involvement in the dramatic arts on the grounds that these are simply "worldly amusements." But James is warning against worldliness *wherever* it is found, certainly in the church, and he is emphasizing here precisely the importance of Christian involvement in *social* issues. Regrettably, we tend to read the Scriptures as though their rejection of a "worldly" life-style entails a recommendation of an "otherworldly" one.

This approach has led many Christians to abandon the "secular" realm to the trends and forces of secularism. Indeed, because of their two-realm theory, to a large degree, Christians have themselves to blame for the rapid secularization of the West. If political, industrial, artistic, and journalistic life, to mention only these areas, are branded as essentially "worldly," "secular," "profane," and part of the "natural domain of creaturely life," then is it surprising that Christians have not more effectively stemmed the tide of humanism in our culture?

The Bible refers to the perversion and distortion of creation with many different words. Besides "world," it uses such terms as "futility," "corruption," and "bondage." "Bondage" is of particular interest for us because it illustrates how the havoc wreaked by mankind is associated with the work of Satan. To sin, in the Bible, is to serve Satan—or rather, to be enslaved to Satan. Outside the service of Yahweh there is only bondage—witting or unwitting slavery to Satan. This is true of creation as a whole. Where the creature does not find its freedom in responding obediently to the Creator's norms, there it enters bondage.

Bondage in Scripture has to do with enslavement to a spiritual empire. The Bible speaks very straightforwardly of the domination of the devil over God's creatures and of the demonic forces that God's people must contend with. Satan stands at the head of a whole hierarchy of evil spirits who seek to twist and spoil the good gifts of the Creator. To the degree that these spirits are successful, creation loses it lustre, becoming ugly rather than beautiful. The world becomes quite literally "demonized." It is in this sense that Scripture calls Satan "the prince of this world" (John 12:31).

Satan's agency raises a problem. If the perversion of creation is rooted in human sinfulness, how can that perversion also be attributed to Satan? Must not the villain be either man or Satan? The Scriptures are perfectly clear on this matter. While constantly linking humanity's disobedience with its allegiance to the powers of darkness, they never diminish mankind's own responsibility. To sin is to be in bondage to Satan, and yet the excuse "the devil made me do it" is never valid. Despite the role played by Satan, it is humanity that bears the blame for making the distorted creation groan. Though something is impenetrable here, as in the question of human responsibility versus God's sovereignty, clarity in biblical teaching is certainly not lacking.

Consider the role of Satan in the biblical story of the fall. The earthly realm is still unaffected by evil when the serpent (embodying the fallen angel from the heavenly realm) entices humankind to sin. Only when mankind sins, and only on that account, is the good earthly realm subjected to futility and bondage. Satan can wreak havoc on the good earth only by first controlling mankind. The earth and its condition is and remains a human responsibility.

The sum total of evil and rottenness in creation (i.e., "the world") is therefore the result of both human sin and the creature's enslavement to the devil. This link between "evil" and "enslavement" is very foreign to the modern mind because of our pride in human autonomy and freedom. Yet this association is obvious in the Scriptures and was accepted without question by Christians for many centuries. A curious and instructive relic of this earlier easy identification of evil and bondage is preserved in the Italian language. The common Italian word for "bad" or "evil" is *cattivo*, which is the direct descendant of the Latin *captivus* (*diaboli*), "captive (to the devil)." This derivation reflects a genuine understanding of the Bible's teaching concerning the ultimately spiritual nature of all evil.

We should also add that at times what we have said about "world" and "worldly" fits the scriptural usage of "earth" and "earthly." When Paul enjoins us to put to death the "members which are upon the earth" (Col. 3:5, KJV), indentifying these as "fornication, uncleanness, inordinate affection, evil concupiscence," and the like, and when he says of the enemies of the cross that "their mind is on earthly things" (Phil. 3:19), he clearly refers to the fallen and corrupted earth, not to the earth that was declared "very good" in Genesis 1. And since it was the earth, not heaven, that was infected by sin, he can present the exhortation to "Set your mind on things above, not on earthly things" (Col. 3:2). Paul does not mean that such earthly things as sexuality and sports and carpentry are evil in themselves (they are in fact part of God's good creation); he means that they are corrupted and polluted compared to the perfection of God's dwelling place. To them too we must apply the petition "Thy will be done on earth as in heaven."

To summarize, we have seen that the fall affects the whole range of earthly creation; that sin is a parasite on, and not a part of, creation; and that, to the degree that it affects the whole earth, sin profanes all things, making them "worldly," "secular," "earthly." Consequently, every area of the created world cries out for redemption and the coming of the kingdom of God.

4

Redemption

We have seen how the concept of creation must be taken much more broadly than Christians ordinarily take it, and how mankind's fall into sin affects the entire range of that broadly conceived creation. All of this has been preparation for making the basic point that the redemption achieved by Jesus Christ is *cosmic* in the sense that it restores the whole creation.

This fundamental confession has two distinct parts. The first is that redemption means *restoration*—that is, the return to the goodness of an originally unscathed creation and not merely the addition of something supracreational. The second is that this restoration affects the *whole* of creational life and not merely some limited area within it. Both of these affirmations are crucial to an integral biblical worldview, and both are pregnant with important consequences for Christian discipleship.

Salvation as Restoration

It is quite striking that virtually all of the basic words describing salvation in the Bible imply a *return* to an originally good state or situation. *Redemption* is a good example. To redeem is to "buy free," literally to "buy back," and the image it evokes is that of a kidnapping. A free person has been seized and is being held for ransom. Someone else pays the ransom on behalf of the captive and thus "buys back" his or her original freedom. The point of redemption is to free the prisoner from bondage, to give back the freedom he or she once enjoyed. Something similar can be said about *reconciliation*, in which, again, the prefix *re-* indicates going back to an original state. Here the image is that of friends who have fallen out, or former allies who have declared war on one another. They have become reconciled and return to their original friendship and alliance. Another salvation word beginning with re- is *renewal*—in fact Paul uses the comparable prefix *ana-* to coin the Greek word *anakainosis* when he speaks of "the *renewal* of your mind" in Romans 12:2. Literally, this word means "a making new again." What was once brand new but has gotten worse for wear is now re- novated, brought back to its former newness. Still another is the Greek word for "salvation" itself: *sōteria* generally has the meaning "health" or "security" after sickness or danger. As a matter of fact, the first English translation of the Greek New Testament, published by William Tyndale in 1525, regularly renders this word as "health." Christ is the great physician who heals our sickness unto death and restores us to health. Finally, the key biblical concept of "regeneration" implies a return to life after the entrance of death. All these terms suggest a *restoration* of some good thing that was spoiled or lost.

Acknowledging this scriptural emphasis, theologians have sometimes spoken of salvation as "re-creation"—not to imply that God scraps his earlier creation and in Jesus Christ makes a new one, but rather to suggest that he hangs on to his fallen original creation and *salvages* it. He refuses to abandon the work of his hands—in fact he sacrifices his own Son to save his original project. Humankind, which has botched its original mandate and the whole creation along with it, is given another chance in Christ; we are reinstated as God's managers on earth. The original good creation is to be restored.

The practical implications of that intention are legion. Marriage should not be avoided by Christians, but sanctified. Emotions should not be repressed, but purified. Sexuality is not simply to be shunned, but redeemed. Politics should not be declared off-limits, but reformed. Art ought not to be pronounced worldly, but claimed for Christ. Business must no longer be relegated to the secular world, but must be made to conform again to God-honoring standards. Every sector of human life yields such examples.

In a very significant sense this restoration means that salvation does not bring anything new. Redemption is not a matter of an addition of a spiritual or supernatural dimension to creaturely life that was lacking before; rather, it is a matter of bringing new life and vitality to what was there all along. It is true enough, of course, that the whole drama of salvation brings elements into the picture that were not part of God's creational design (think for example of the regulations that were necessitated by sin: capital punishment, divorce legislation, cities of refuge, and so on). But like scaffolding attached to a house being renovated, or bandages covering a wound, these are all incidental to the main purpose, meant only to serve the process of restoration. In fact, once that purpose is served, they are discardable. It would be foolish to say that medical treatment aims at more than the restoration of health because it brings medicines, bandages, and stethoscopes into the picture. By the same token, salvation brings many things into the lives of God's people that are not solely part of the restoration of creation, and yet that restoration is nonetheless the exclusive focus of redemption. At bottom, the only thing redemption adds that is not included in the creation is the remedy for sin, and that remedy is brought in solely for the purpose of recovering a sinless creation. To put it in the traditional language of theology, grace does not bring a *donum superadditum* to nature, a gift added on top of creation; rather, grace *restores* nature, making it whole once more.

If salvation does not bring more than creation, it does not bring less either. It is *all* of creation that is included in the scope of Christ's redemption: that scope is truly cosmic. Through Christ, God determined "to reconcile to himself *all things,*" writes Paul (Col. 1:20), and the words he uses (*ta panta*) preclude any narrow or personalistic understanding of the reconciliation he has in mind. It may seem strange to us that the apostle uses the word *reconcile* in this connection, when he has more than human beings in mind, but this usage simply confirms what we have learned about the scope of the fall: "all things" are drawn into the mutiny of the human race and its enmity toward God, and their strained relations with the Creator must be "patched up," brought once more into harmony with him. The scope of redemption is as great as that of the fall; it embraces creation as a whole. the root cause of all evil on earth—namely, the sin of the human race—is atoned for and overcome in Christ's death and resurrection, and therefore in principle his redemption also removes all of sin's effects. Wherever there is disruption of the good creation—and that disruption, as we saw, is unrestricted in its scope—there Christ provides the possibility of restoration. If the whole creation is affected by the fall, then the whole creation is also reclaimed in Christ.

We touch here upon the essential point where the reformational worldview differs from other worldviews in the tradition of historic Christian orthodoxy. What distinguishes a reformational worldview is its understanding of the radical and universal import of both sin and redemption. There is something totalitarian about the claims of both Satan and Christ; nothing in all of creation is neutral in the sense that it is untouched by the dispute between these two great adversaries.

The biblical accounts of sin and redemption are similar on another point. In both cases, although the whole creation is involved, it is still *humanity* that plays the pivotal role. Just as the fall of man (Adam) was the ruin of the whole earthly realm, so the atoning death of a man (Jesus Christ, the second Adam) is the salvation of the whole world. Likewise, just as the first Adam's fall was aided and abetted by the subsequent disobedience of humankind, so the salvation of the whole world is manifested and promoted by the subsequent obedience of a new humankind. The Adamic human race perverts the cosmos; the Christian human race renews it.

The obvious implication is that the new humanity (God's people) is called to promote renewal in every department of creation. If Christ is the reconciler of all things, and if we have been entrusted with "the ministry of reconciliation" on his behalf (2 Cor. 5:18), then we have a redemptive task wherever our vocation places us in his world. No invisible dividing line within creation limits the applicability of such basic biblical concepts as reconciliation, redemption, salvation, sanctification, renewal, the kingdom of God, and so on. In the name of Christ, distortion must be opposed *everywhere*—in the kitchen and the bedroom, in city councils and corporate boardrooms, on the stage and on the air, in the classroom and in the workshop. Everywhere creation calls for the honoring of God's standards. Everywhere humanity's sinfulness disrupts and deforms. Everywhere Christ's victory is pregnant with the defeat of sin and the recovery of creation.

The Kingdom of God

That salvation means the restoration of creation can be illustrated by a discussion of the kingdom of God, for in fact the restoration in Christ of creation and the coming of the kingdom of God are one and the same. let us begin by specifying the meaning of the word *kingdom*. The Greek word *basileia*, which is usually translated as "kingdom," means in the first place "kingship"—that is to say, "sovereignty," "sway," "dominion." It refers not so much to an area or domain (though this is a possible denotation) as to the active exercise of the kingly office. The emphasis is on God as he is active in his sovereign ruling as king. When Jesus tells the parable of the nobleman who goes to a far country to "receive for himself a kingdom" (Luke 19:12, KJV), he is thinking of a ruler like Herod or Archelaus who had to travel to the emperor in Rome to "have himself appointed king." The kingdom of God, therefore, calls to mind the rightful king as he rules his territory, creation.

Although God is often pictured as the king of heaven and earth in the Old Testament, this theme becomes particularly prominent in the New Testament. Herman Ridderbos, author of the excellent study *The Coming of the Kingdom*, has said that the kingdom of God is "the central theme of the whole New Testament revelation of God." In Jesus Christ we witness the long-awaited vindication and effective demonstration of God's kingship in the world. The coming of Christ is the climax of the whole history of redemption as recorded in the Scriptures. The rightful king has established a beachhead in his territory and calls on his subjects to press his claims ever farther in creation.

Jesus' Ministry

Jesus' ministry clearly demonstrates that the coming of the kingdom means the restoration of creation. Christ's work was not only a preaching of the long-awaited coming of the kingdom, but also a *demonstration* of that coming. In his words and especially in his deeds Jesus himself was proof that the kingdom had arrived. After casting an evil spirit out of a blind and mute man, Jesus says to the Pharisees, "If I drive out demons by the Spirit of God, then the kingdom of God has come upon you" (Matt. 12:28).

Jesus' miracles, therefore, not only attest to the truth of his preaching concerning the coming of the kingdom but actually demonstrate that coming. Christ's healing constituted actual evidence of his kingship over the power of sickness and Satan. In connection

with our theme of re-creation it is particularly striking that all of
Jesus' miracles (with the one exception of the cursing of the fig
tree) are miracles of *restoration*—restoration to health, restoration
to life, restoration to freedom from demonic possession. Jesus' miracles provide us with a sample of the meaning of redemption: a
freeing of creation from the shackles of sin and evil and a reinstate-
ment of creaturely living as intended by God.

It was a demonstration of the coming of the kingdom when Jesus
said to the woman who had been crippled for eighteen years,
"Woman, you are set free from your infirmity" (Luke 13:12), and
the woman immediately straightened up. This healing was at the
same time a confrontation of the liberating King with the enslaving
usurper, for Jesus himself adds that the woman was one "whom
Satan has kept bound for eighteen long years" (v. 16). That the
healings were a contest with Satan is clear from the link between
sickness and possession in many of Jesus' signs and wonders, and
from the way Peter summarizes Christ's ministry to Cornelius: "He
went around doing good and healing all who were under the power
of the devil" (Acts 10:38). The story of the Gadarene demoniac is
another instance in which the healing by Jesus is striking evidence
of the coming of the kingdom. The demon in the possessed man
fell at Jesus' feet (in recognition of his divinity and kingship), addressed him as "Son of the Most High God," and then begged him
not to punish it (Luke 8:28). This response on the part of the evil
spirit shows that the King is acknowledged, that his superior power
is feared, and that the presence of the kingdom is recognized. Jesus
himself, when asked by the messengers of John the Baptist whether
he really was the long-awaited messianic king, replied that his ministry spoke for itself: "Go back and report to John what you hear
and see: The blind receive sight, the lame walk, those who have
leprosy are cured, the deaf hear, the dead are raised, and good news
is preached to the poor" (Matt. 11:4-5). The healing, restoring
work of Christ marks the invasion of the kingdom into the fallen
creation.

So, in the person of Jesus the kingdom of God is already present.
When the Pharisees asked him when the kingdom would come,
Jesus answered, "In fact the Kingdom of God is among you" (Luke
17:21, NEB). And yet he also instructed his disciples to pray "Thy
kingdom come," and taught that its coming is *not yet* an accom-

plished reality. Both the "already" and the "not yet" aspects characterize the interlude between Christ's first and second coming. The first coming establishes his foothold in creation, while the second coming accomplishes the complete victory of his sovereignty. In the meantime, his servants are called to honor that sovereignty everywhere, for it is already true that "all authority in heaven and on earth" has been given to him (Matt. 28:18). Since his ascension Jesus has continued to make his kingdom come, but now by means of the ministry of his followers empowered by the Holy Spirit. This is the point of the parable of the pounds (Luke 19:11-27), in which the nobleman's servants are called to be faithful in their assigned tasks before the nobleman returns from receiving the kingship. The servants of the already-come kingdom invest their entire resources for the promotion of the kingdom not-yet-come.

Concretely, this parable means that in the name of Christ and his kingdom Christians must now employ all their God-given means in opposing the sickness and demonization of creation—and thus in restoring creation—in anticipation of its final "regeneration" at the second coming (Matt. 19:28). This directive holds for our private lives (e.g., in such things as keeping promises, helping friends, practicing hospitality) but also for such public endeavors as work in advertising, labor-management relations, education, and international affairs. Christ lays his claim upon it all; nothing is excluded from the scope of his kingship. Those who refuse to honor that kingship are like the nobleman's countrymen who declared "We don't want this man to be our king" (Luke 19:14).

One should not think that the scriptural emphasis on restoration implies that Christians should advocate a return to the garden of Eden, however. We have already noted that creation develops through culture and society and that this development is good and healthy. Part of God's plan for the earth is that it be filled and subdued by humankind, that its latent possibilities be unlocked and actualized in human history and civilization. A good deal of that development has already taken place, though it is distorted by humanity's sinfulness.

We must choose *restoration* rather than *repristination*. It would be a profound mistake to attempt to go back to the original stage of the earth's development, to the sort of world exemplified by the garden of Eden. From a cultural point of view, that situation was primitive and undeveloped. It preceded Jabal, Jubal, and Tubal Cain (sons of Lamech), for example, who introduced a number of historical advances (animal husbandry, music making, metalworking) that contributed significantly to the furtherance of civilization (see Gen. 4:20-22). It is doubtful whether Adam and Eve were acquainted with the wheel; it is certain that they had not yet discovered how to make textiles (Gen. 3:21) or bake bricks (Gen. 11:3). In the language of modern archaeology, they lived in the early Stone Age. Repristination would entail the *cultural* return to the garden of Eden, a return that would turn back the historical clock. Such a move would be historically reactionary or regressive.

That is not the meaning of restoration in Jesus Christ. In the terms of the analogy of the teenager who had been sick since babyhood, a return to health at a later stage of development would not entail a return to the stage of physical development that characterized the youth's earlier period of good health. Genuine healing for the youth would be a matter of a healthy progression through adolescence to adulthood. By analogy, salvation in Jesus Christ, conceived in the broad creational sense, means a restoration of culture and society in their present stage of development. That restoration will not necessarily oppose literacy or urbanization or industrialization or the internal combustion engine, although these historical developments have led to their own distortions or evils. Instead, the coming of the kingdom of God demands that these developments be reformed, that they be made answerable to their creational structure, and that they be subjected to the ordinances of the Creator.

Biblical religion is historically progressive, not reactionary. It views the whole course of history as a movement from a garden to a city, and it fundamentally affirms that movement. Once again, the kingdom of God claims *all* of creation, not only in all its departments, but also in all its stages of development.

Comparison with Other Views of the Kingdom

It is clear that the conception of the kingdom of God outlined here differs from that of Christians with other worldviews. It is probably safe to say that our view of the extent of the kingdom constitutes as telling an index of our worldview as does our conception of "the world." An almost ineradicable tendency exists among Christians to restrict the scope of the kingdom—a tendency that parallels the persistent inclination to divide the world into sacred and profane realms.

Perhaps the most common example of this restriction in Protestantism is found in *pietism*. Pietists restrict the kingdom of God to the sphere of personal piety, the inner life of the soul. They prefer to translate Luke 17:21 as "behold, the kingdom of God is *within* you" (KJV) rather than "*among* you" (NEB).

Other traditions curtail the scope of Christ's kingship by identifying the kingdom with the institutional church. Though this identification is traditionally thought of as being Roman Catholic, its Protestant adherents are numerous. This view holds that only clergymen and missionaries engage in "full-time kingdom work" and that the laity are involved in kingdom activity only to the degree that they are engaged in church work. This restriction has given rise to the misleading phrase "church and world," which suggests that all of human affairs are in fact divided into two spheres.

By contrast, the dispensationalists restrict the kingdom to the eschatological future. For them the petition "Thy kingdom come" means "May the millennium not be long in coming." This view strictly equates the kingdom and the millennium and holds that neither of them is in any way "already present."

Classical liberal Protestantism (the social gospel, for example), on the other hand, attaches the name "kingdom of God" to anything that seems humane and progressive from a humanistic point of view. Liberal democracy or the American way of life are seen as coterminous with Christ's kingship by adherents of this view, and any countermovement is considered secular by definition. Much of contemporary liberation theology is similar, though it sees the kingdom manifested not so much in liberal as in Marxist sociopolitical movements.

All these examples illustrate that the permanent temptation of Christian thinking is to find new variants of a two-realm theory that restricts the scope of Christ's lordship. Again and again Christians find ways of excluding certain areas or dimensions of their lives and the life of their culture from the need for reform for Christ's sake. Again and again we must remind ourselves that Christ is not satisfied with halfway measures, that he reclaims all of creational life. What we are here calling the reformational worldview is an attempt to honor, in an explicit and consistent way, the insistent message of Scripture that sin is radical, deep, and pervasive. Christ is a match—more than a match—for Satan throughout creation. Satan has done his worst, but Christ has bested him.

Perhaps a diagram can illustrate the decisive difference between the different worldviews of Christendom. Let us imagine that a square represents creation in all its variety and extent. In a rough and ready way, we shall divide the square into some of the creation's major areas (see Figure A, below). It is important to note that the lines separating the different areas represent or approximate real distinctions drawn by the *Creator*, not by the fall or some arbitrary human convention. Church life is different in kind from family life, because God created the church and the family unique and different. Both thought and emotion, for example, have their own specific natures—that is, each is created "after its kind" (Gen. 1:11ff.). The lines dividing different kinds of creatures are God-ordained and good.

Figure A

church
family
politics
business
art
education
journalism
thought
emotion
plants and animals
inanimate matter

A two-realm theory supposes that there is a line dividing creation into two realms, and it typically identifies that line with one of the creationally given "seams" separating different kinds of creaturely activity. One commonly made separation is indicated by Figure B (see page 68). The line in this figure separating the kingdom of God and the church from "the world" may be placed at a different level (the kingdom might include family life, for example, or work done in a Christian hospital or school), but the division is horizontal and drawn along creational lines.

The Scriptures present matters in a much different light. Both God and Satan lay claim to the *whole* of creation, leaving nothing neutral or undisputed. The scriptural diagram looks something like that outlined in Figure C (see page 68), in which the contrast is not between two realms but between two regimes. The dividing line between them cuts across every creational reality; it nowhere coincides with legitimate creaturely differences. The line is jagged rather than straight because it represents the battle line between forces of the opposing regimes, and different areas experience varying degrees of liberation or bondage. Moreover, the line *moves*: wherever family life, for example, grows in obedience and conformity to God's creational law, there the kingdom advances and the world is pushed back. Wherever the spirit of humanism secularizes human thought, there the kingdom of God loses terrain and is taken captive "through hollow and deceptive philosophy, which depends on human tradition and the basic principles of this world rather than on Christ" (Col. 2:8). It is even possible that I might experience dramatic liberation by Christ in one part of my life (my emotions, perhaps, or my family life) while another remains sadly secular (my thinking, for example, or my church involvement). The same disparity can hold true of particular nations or traditions. The opposition between light and dark, life and death, wisdom and folly, health and sickness, obedience and disobedience manifests itself everywhere. Nothing is "neutral" in the sense that sin fails to affect it or that redemption fails to hold out the promise of deliverance.

This radical dividing line between the two kingdoms is the same line that divides "the flesh" and "the spirit" in the individual human being, or "the old man" and "the new man." One of the great advances of the Reformation was its insight that "flesh" and "spirit" in the New Testament do not correspond to the "body" and "soul"

Figure B

the kingdom of God (sacred)	church
	family
	politics
	business
	art
"the world" (secular)	education
	journalism
	thought
	emotion
	plants and animals
	inanimate matter

Figure C

	chu rch	
	fami ly	
	poli tics	
	bu siness	
the kingdom of God	ar t	"the world"
	edu cation	
	journali sm	
	thou ght	
	em otion	
	plants and animals	
	inanimate matter	

of pagan Greek philosophy, but divide them both. In his commentary on Galatians 5, Luther exclaims on the works of the flesh and the fruit of the spirit: *totus homo caro*—"the whole person is flesh!" In that one statement Luther replaces a straight line with a jagged vertical one. The temptation to categorize the creation into good and bad areas must be resisted. The works of the flesh are not just bodily sins (Paul included idolatry and hatred in his list), nor is the fruit of the Spirit only "mental"; the whole person is claimed by each contending force. Again, these forces stand in stark opposition to each other: the flesh and the Spirit "are contrary the one to the other," writes Paul (Gal. 5:17, KJV) using a Greek verb related to *antithesis*. The Spirit, which is the Spirit of holiness, opposes distortion in order to reaffirm and glorify God's original creative intent.

Redemption, then, is the recovery of creational goodness through the annulment of sin and the effort toward the progressive removal of its effects everywhere. We return to creation through the cross, because only the atonement deals with sin and evil effectively at their root. Mark's version of the great commission bids us "preach the good news to *all creation*" (Mark 16:15) because there is need of liberation from sin everywhere.

An Illustration

A simple illustration can clarify the overall biblical conception of creation, fall, and redemption. We have noted that the Scriptures speak of the human condition as the battle between two kingdoms— the kingdom of Satan (or "the world" in its negative sense) and the kingdom of Christ. Being a Christian means that God "has rescued us from the dominion of darkness [i.e., the kingdom of Satan] and brought us into the kingdom of the Son he loves" (Col. 1:13). Involved in the dispute between these two kingdoms are two sovereigns who contend for the same territory and who lead two opposing armies into the field. Each army owes allegiance to one of the sovereigns. The territory in dispute, the creation of God, has been invaded by God's adversary, Satan, who now holds creation as an occupied territory with military force. In Jesus Christ God launches a counteroffensive to reclaim his rightful domain. By the death and resurrection of Jesus Christ the victory has in principle been achieved. God has established a beachhead in creation and has staked out his claim for the whole. We now live in the period between the decisive battle, won by Christ, and the definitive establishment of his sovereignty over all of his territories. The warfare that still rages between the soldiers of Christ and the agents of Satan has the character of a mop-up operation.

In his book *Christ and Time*, Swiss theologian Oscar Cullmann writes of the Normandy invasion of 1944 in relation to the end of the Second World War. That invasion, occurring on "D-Day," was necessary before "V-Day," the actual moment of final and complete victory. The death and resurrection of Jesus Christ, says Cullmann, are like D-Day, and Christ's second coming and the last judgment will be like V-Day. We now live in the times between, assured of victory but still fighting a fierce battle.

Let us look at the basic elements of this military metaphor. The chief protagonists are two kings, one legitimate and the other a usurper, each having his own sovereignty and army, each waging war for the possession of the same territory. The kingship of the rightful sovereign is what the Bible calls "the kingdom of God" while that of his rival is called "the world" or the kingdom of darkness. The Scriptures call one of the armies "the people of God" ("the church" in the New Testament) and the other "those outside"—that is, all of mankind outside Christ and in bondage to Satan. The battle between the sovereignties is what Abraham Kuyper called the "antithesis," the spiritual warfare between God and Satan. Finally, the territory that both sovereigns dispute between them is the whole domain of creation. Each lays claim to the totality of the created order.

The Bible abounds in imagery drawn from this military picture. Think of Paul's account of spiritual warfare in Ephesians 6, or of his warning against being taken prisoner of war by philosophy in Colossians 2, or of his comparison of evangelism with a siege in 2 Corinthians 10:3-6. The book of Revelation, too, draws heavily on this kind of image, picturing vividly the cosmic battle between the Lamb and the dragon and utilizing the Old Testament conception of God as warrior. Christians today tend to be shy of such terminology, finding it too militaristic. And indeed it is true that there are real dangers here. We all know how easy it is to turn the Bible's call to spiritual warfare into support for the sort of misguided Christian patriotism that identifies the geopolitical interests of a particular state with the cause of the kingdom of God. Yet we must take Scripture on its own terms and seek to understand what the Spirit means by using the language of warfare.

A genuinely biblical worldview recognizes that a real battle rages between God and his adversary for the control of creation. This is a spiritual battle, to be sure, but scarcely less serious on that account. Perhaps the battle surfaces most dramatically in cases of demon possession and exorcism, both in biblical times and today. But the confrontation is no less real when less naked and overt, as in the progressive secularization of mass media, medical ethics, and public education. This spiritual warfare hits many bright Christian students hard when they make the transition from high school to university or college. Unless they have an integral biblical world-view that equips them to fight back with the sword of the Spirit, their alternatives are either to live a life of almost intolerable intellectual schizophrenia (the chapel hermetically sealed off from the classroom) or to be swept along in the maelstrom of secular humanism. Paul's warning is as applicable now as nineteen centuries ago: "See to it that no one takes you captive through hollow and deceptive philosophy, which depends on human tradition and the basic principles of this world rather than on Christ" (Col. 2:8). Tragically, the battle for creation still has its casualties.

The sum of our discussion of a reformational worldview is simply this: (1) creation is much broader and more comprehensive than we tend to think, (2) the fall affects that creation in its full extent, and (3) redemption in Jesus Christ reaches just as far as the fall. The horizon of creation is at the same time the horizon of sin and of salvation. To conceive of either the fall or Christ's deliverance as encompassing less that the whole of creation is to compromise the biblical teaching of the radical nature of the fall and the cosmic scope of redemption.

5

Discerning Structure and Direction

In a few bold strokes we have sketched the outline of a biblical worldview, stressing the breadth and range of creation and the effects of sin and salvation on that creation in its full extent. We have seen that these central realities—creation, fall, redemption—are the fundamental points of the biblical compass. When we look through the corrective lens of Scripture, everywhere the things of our experience begin to reveal themselves as *creaturely*, as under the curse of *sin*, and as longing for *redemption*. These are the ABC's of authentically Christian experience, the biblical assumptions that clarify our experience when we bring every thought into obedience in Jesus Christ.

In this chapter we will look at some of the practical *implications* of this worldview for the societal, personal, and cultural lives of Christians. Drawing from a wide range of examples, we shall examine how creation, fall, and redemption—or "structure" and "direction," our shorthand notation for these biblical themes—ought to shape the convictions of a biblical people. How, for example, should Christians today make sense of the conflicting opinions about technology, or aggression, or political revolution, or dance, or education, or sexuality? Does our examination of the nature of creation, fall, and redemption bear any fruit for a biblical approach to these affairs?

We shall argue that in all cases the task of the Christian is to discern *structure* and *direction*. As we have noted, *structure* denotes the "essence" of a creaturely thing, the kind of creature it is by virtue of God's creational law. *Direction*, by contrast, refers to a sinful deviation from that structural ordinance and renewed conformity to it in Christ. A reformational analysis of every area of life will apply this biblical distinction consistently. It will place equal emphasis on creation (structure) and on the spiritual antithesis (direction) pervading all of creation.

When we use the distinction between structure and direction, we must always bring them together under the theme of "grace restores nature." It is not enough simply to say that creational ordinances or structures hold for reality everywhere and that a religious conflict is at work in that reality. No, we must say that the religious conflict rages *for the sake* of the created structure. The everyday components of our lives—our family, our sexuality, our thinking, our emotions, our work—are the structural things that are *involved* and *at stake* in the pull of sin and grace. The directional battle does not take place on a spiritual plane above creaturely reality but rather occurs *in* and *for* the concrete reality of the earthly creation. This basic connection I take to be the genius of a fully biblical vision of what life and the world are all about. All of our lives, and all of the realities of our daily experience, are constituted by structure and direction, the basic ingredients of life.

This twin emphasis makes a radical difference in the way Christian believers approach reality. Because they believe that creational structure underlies all of reality, they seek and find evidence of lawful constancy in the flux of experience, and of invariant principles amidst a variety of historical events and institutions. Because they confess that a spiritual direction underlies their experience, they see abnormality where others see normality, and possibilities of renewal where others see inevitable distortion. In every situation, they explicitly look for and recognize the presence of creational structure, distinguishing this sharply from the human abuse to which it is subject. Their sensitivities are everywhere attuned to creation and antithesis, the two foundational realities that the Scriptures so clearly and consistently teach and that the religion of modern humanism so clearly and consistently denies.

Reformation

The first implication of the reformational worldview is very broad and underlies all the others. It describes the basic temper and attitude that should accompany the Christian as he or she tackles the societal, personal, and cultural issues of the day. We can derive this implication from the word *reformation*, the noun at the root of *reformational*. A number of overtones to this word are part of the perspective we are outlining. The obvious first one is the Reformation itself, the sixteenth-century revival of biblical religion. Certainly the perspective we are calling reformational is rooted firmly in this pivotal movement, which we believe was based on a rediscovery of the Word of God. But two other connotations of "reformation" are also present in the term *reformational*, connotations it will be useful to explain at greater length.

The first is this: reformation means *sanctification*, not *consecration*. Both words mean "making holy," but they are not strictly synonymous. *To sanctify* (or *hallow*, to use an Anglo-Saxon word) means "to make free from sin, to cleanse from moral corruption, to purify." *To consecrate*, on the other hand, generally means simply "to set apart, to dedicate, to devote to the service or worship of God." Consecration therefore means *external* renewal; sanctification means *internal* renewal. The word *reformation* refers to sanctification in this sense of inner revitalization.

It is clearly sanctification that is meant when we speak of the restoration of creation through the death and resurrection of Jesus Christ. Sanctification is the process whereby the Holy Spirit, in and through the people of God, purifies creation from sin on the basis of Christ's atonement and victory. That purifying activity, that making holy, is a process that brings an inner renewal and revitalization of God's creatures, not just an external connection to the institutional church and its services of worship. The "Spirit of holiness" seeks to permeate our creaturely lives, making a qualitative difference in the internal workings of family, business, art, government, and so on.

A dualistic worldview—one that sees a basic division between sacred and secular, holy and profane—restricts sanctification and the work of the Spirit to the sacred and holy realm (usually the institutional church) and allows only "consecration" (some external connection with the sacred) for the rest of life. In certain Roman Catholic circles, for example, a car, or a barn, or even a new business enterprise may be consecrated by having the priest, the representative of the church, sprinkle holy water on it. Or the institution of marriage may be "made holy" by having it declared a sacrament or by holding the wedding in a church. Only through such a sacramental "elevation" of the things in the natural world do these Christians feel that they can bring secular affairs into contact with the grace of God. But this consecration is a far cry from the inner sanctification of business or marital life that the Bible calls for. If these areas of creation are to be truly restored, they must be made holy from within, in terms of what they uniquely are: there must, for example, be economic holiness in business and marital holiness in marriage. The renewing power of salvation in Jesus Christ penetrates the very fabric of the "natural world," hallowing it from within.

This holiness is what the apostle Paul had in mind when he wrote so emphatically to Timothy that everything created by God (he explicitly includes marriage) is "sanctified" by the Word of God and prayer (1 Tim. 4:5). The Revised Standard Version and the New International Version are wrong to change *sanctified* (the word found in all major English versions since Tyndale) to *consecrated*, thereby obscuring the basic worldview instruction that Paul is giving. There is no doubt that in this passage and in the New Testament generally, Paul uses the Greek word *hagiazein* (literally, "to make holy") to refer to internal renewal and purification from the pollution of sin. There is nothing superficial about the work of the Spirit.

Jesus makes exactly the same point in one of his parables, the shortest on record. "The kingdom of heaven," he said, "is like yeast that a woman took and mixed into a large amount of flour until it worked all through the dough" (Matt. 13:33). We learn from this that the gospel is a leavening influence in human life wherever it is lived, an influence that slowly but steadily brings change from within. The gospel affects government in a specifically political manner, art in a peculiarly aesthetic manner, scholarship in a uniquely theoretical manner, and churches in a distinctly ecclesiastical manner. It makes possible a renewal of each creational area from *within*, not without.

The conception of sanctification, or of hallowing, as a process of progressive inner renewal in every phase of human life (not just in the context of worship activities) is a unique feature of biblical religion. In all other religions it seems that the holy belongs only to the realm of the cult, to the domain of the temple, the priest, sacrifices, and so on. Everything outside that realm is considered "profane" or "unclean." The New Testament changes this radically: for Paul, "nothing is unclean in itself" (Rom. 14:14), and every created thing can be made holy. This had already been predicted in the Old Testament: "On that day HOLY TO THE LORD will be inscribed on the bells of the horses. . . . Every pot in Jerusalem and Judah will be holy to the LORD almighty" (Zech. 14:20-21). "Holiness" in the New Testament is not restricted to the cult but characterizes the entire life of God's people—private and public, personal and cultural. Pentecost means not only that the Spirit comes to renew human life from within but also that this sanctifying renewal spreads to the full range of human activities. Everything in principle can be sanctified and internally renewed—our personal life, our societal relationships, our cultural activities. There is no limit to the scope of the hallowing operation of the Holy Spirit. How significant it is that the cultic terminology of the Old Testament (e.g., temple, sacrifice, priesthood, incense) is transferred in the New either to Christ or to the entire life of his body, the Church!

So reformation means in the first place sanctification. A second feature of reformation is that the avenue of this sanctification is *progressive renewal* rather than *violent overthrow*. This principle is particularly relevant on a societal and cultural plane, for it offers a biblical strategy for historical change. How ought Christians to confront minimalist art, or computer technology, or liberation theology, or recent trends in journalism? In the light of our worldview, it is clear that God calls his people to a *historical reformation* in all these areas, to a sanctification of creational realities from sin and its effects. What was *formed* in creation has been historically *deformed* by sin and must be *reformed* in Christ.

Negatively speaking, we may define this strategy by contrasting *reformation* with *revolution* in the modern political sense. The Dutch tradition of reformational thinking has regularly opposed reformation to the French Revolution of 1789, the later revolutions of 1848, and the revolution preached by orthodox Marxists. But we may just as easily contrast reformation with the revolution advocated today by neo-Marxists and others in various parts of the world.

When we use *revolution* in this basically negative sense, we do not mean that anything designated as a revolution is by that fact bad. Some may say that the discovery of penicillin caused a "revolution" in medicine. But the word then simply means something like "dramatic change for the better" and is perfectly acceptable. In fact, the term has become so overused (think of the ads that recommend a "revolutionary" new toothpaste) that its original connotation of a vast and sweeping upheaval has been greatly watered down. In the present context, however, we are thinking of the political meanings that the word first acquired in the late eighteenth century, perhaps best exemplified by the political upheavals in 1789 and 1918.

Revolution in this sense is characterized by the following features, among others: (1) necessary violence, (2) the complete removal of every aspect of the established system, and (3) the construction of an entirely different societal order according to a theoretical ideal. The biblical principle of "reformation" opposes each of these three points. In the first place, reformation stresses the necessity of avoiding violence both in the ordinary sense of harming individuals with physical or psychological force and in the historical sense of wrenching and dislocating the social fabric. No matter how dramatic the new life in Jesus Christ may be, it does not seek to tear the fabric of a given historical situation. In the second place—and this is of particular importance—it recognizes that no given societal order is *absolutely* corrupt; thus, no societal order need ever be totally condemned. And in the third place, it does not place its confidence in blueprints and conceptions of the ideal society that have been arrived at by scientific or pseudo-scientific speculation. Instead, it takes the given historical situation as its point of departure, mindful of the apostolic injunction to "test everything [and] hold fast to what is good" (1 Thess. 5:21).

How is this idea of progressive renewal an implication of the worldview we have sketched thus far? It should be clear that our equal stress on structure and direction compels us to choose the attitude of reformation. Structure implies that in some sense every circumstance or condition participates in the creational possibilities God holds out to his creatures in his law. Nothing moves or exists or develops except in response to God's creational demands. God's ordinances make themselves felt in even the most perverse human distortion. As a result some element in every situation is worth preserving. Conversely, everything in reality falls within the scope of religious direction: everything that exists is susceptible to sinful distortion and is in need of religious renewal. Since both the created order and human perversion or renewal are present in any historical situation—and specifically in a cultural or societal establishment— a Christian's rejection of evil must always lead to a cleansing and reforming of created structures, not to an indiscriminate abolition of an entire historical situation.

On the positive side, reformation entails that the normative elements in any distorted situation (and *every* situation is distorted to some extent) should be sought out as a point of contact in terms of which renewal can take place. To reform means to attach oneself to those features of an established order that reflect some normativity and obedience to creational law. Hence, reformation always takes as its point of departure what is historically given and seeks to build on the good rather than clearing the historical terrain radically in order to lay an altogether new foundation. As a practical matter, the holding power of God's law ensures that no human situation can ever be utterly desperate. This is true not only on the personal level but also on the plane of societal reality.

It is evident that this approach emphasizes the positive aspects of tradition, of authority, and of historical continuity. For this reason, the reformational worldview stands in some danger of being perceived as conservatism, as support for the status quo. Such a perception is of course profoundly mistaken, since reformation is inherently and by definition a call for reform. While our emphasis on the constant presence of creational structure rejects a sweeping condemnation of any distorted cultural situation as a whole, the fact that we place an equal emphasis on direction—that is, on the far-reaching and profoundly distorting influences of human perversity as well as on the victorious power of salvation in Jesus Christ— implies that every situation calls for a crusading activity of societal reformation. The status quo is never acceptable. Every "establishment" needs internal renewal and structural reform. In this sense the Christian may never be satisfied with the achievements of any given economic, or political, or generally cultural state of affairs.

So our focus on structure rejects a sympathy for revolution, and our focus on direction condemns a quietistic conservatism. A program of social action inspired by a reformational vision will never seek to start from scratch or begin with a clean slate. Rather, it will always seek to salvage certain elements of whatever historical situation it confronts—not only because those elements are worth saving, but also because they provide "handles," as it were, for renewal.

For Christians, this renewing orientation is particularly important, since severe social oppression and injustice can easily seduce them into identifying the whole social order ("the Establishment," the "status quo," or "the system") with the "world" in its religiously negative sense. When this fatal identification is made, Christians tend to withdraw from all participation in societal renewal. Under the guise of keeping itself from the "world," the body of Christ then in effect allows the powers of secularization and distortion to dominate the greater part of its life. This is not so much an avoidance of evil as a neglect of duty.

We have discussed reformation and revolution primarily in terms of social and political renewal, but the same principle holds in our personal lives (think of the traditional emphasis on sanctification as growing in grace and as a daily process of renewal), in the ecclesiastical establishment, and in all aspects of human culture. We ought not to respond to a sick church by rejecting it wholesale or by refusing to participate in its life, but by attaching ourselves to and building on the good that can still be found in it. Here too we must "hate what is evil, cling to what is good" (Rom. 12:9). So too for those who work in an academic field. No one in such a position can avoid working within an intellectual tradition (nor should anyone try to). But a tradition always embodies elements both normative and anti-normative, both structural and directional. It is the task of every educator to sift out the valuable insights of a tradition and make them fruitful for further progress as well as to expose and reject the falsehood and illusion within that same tradition. And so one could go on. Whether we work in the arts, business, or the media, the strategy of reformation must always guide us. We must respect the historical givens and without compromise call for reform.

In sum we may say that whereas consecration leaves things internally untouched, and revolution annihilates things, reformation *renews* and *sanctifies* them. God calls us to cleanse and reform all the sectors of our lives.

Societal Renewal

Let us move now to the arena of society at large, to that great variety of human institutions and associations including the family, the school, the state, the church, the business corporation, and so forth. Do the biblical principles of structure and direction and the strategy of reformation offer any guidelines to how Christians ought to understand their task of sanctification in the domain of public life?

Our point of departure will be the discernment of structure and direction. Human society gives evidence that a *structured order* underlies the great diversity of societal forms in different cultures and periods of history. The Creator's sustaining and governing hand is not absent from the many ways in which human beings organize their living together. However society arranges itself, it must always do its arranging in terms of creational givens. That the family consists of at least a father, mother, and children living together in bonds of committed caring is not an arbitrary happenstance; nor is it a mere convention that can be dismissed when it has outlived its usefulness. No, it is rooted in the way a wise Creator made human nature—rooted in the biological, emotional, social, and moral constitution of men and women. There is a design for the family, a basic pattern that allows for variety but also sets certain very definite boundaries. Families as we know them are partially obedient and partially disobedient responses to that basic creational pattern. The creational structure of the family is the inescapable requirement for the existence of families at all, allowing us to recognize the family as a family. The family is a societal institution *established* by God, the Creator.

As we noted in our discussion of creation, the principle that societal institutions are creational applies across the board. Not only the family and marriage (two distinct communities) but also the institutional church (to be distinguished from the church as the body of Christ, which participates in the other societal spheres as well) and the state are divinely instituted. In fact, as we have seen, the New Testament explicitly relates the structures of political authority to God's ordinance in creation (see Rom. 13:1-2 and 1 Pet. 2:13-14). The fact that the Scriptures do not expressly speak of a God-ordained structure for such institutions as the school and the business enterprise does not mean that they are arbitrary and have nothing to do with God-given standards. Our own experience of the creation confirms the general scriptural teaching that God's ordinances apply to all of life. Someone may try to run a school like a business (businessmen on school boards often do), but in the long run such an attempt will prove counterproductive. The creational structure of the school resists being pressed into an alien mold — just as a business resists being run like a family. That resistance is evidence of a creational norm. Ignoring God's good creation in these areas simply does not pay, either educationally or economically.

Like all creatures of God, societal institutions have been created "after their kind." Each institution has its own distinct nature and creational structure. All of us have some intuitive awareness of that nature or structure, an awareness that experience and study sharpen and deepen into practical wisdom. An experienced schoolteacher is likely to sense the normative structure of the school more clearly than the average parent. Someone who has worked for years in a service organization is apt to know the creational contours of that area much better than an academician or politician. Each area of societal organization develops its own widely accepted standards of propriety, and anyone who departs from them earns such labels as "unprofessional" or "unbusinesslike." Such standards always reflect an interpretation (whether accurate or misguided) of the creational ordinance (whether acknowledged or not) that holds for the area in question.

Each societal institution is a positivization of the creational structure that holds uniquely for it. (Unfortuantely, in normal language both the individual institution and its creational nature are often called "structure"; to avoid confusion we will reserve the term *structure* for the creational order that holds for creaturely things—in this case, societal institutions.) As we have already noted, positivization is a matter of putting into practice a creational norm. We saw earlier that part of God's rule over creation takes place through the mediation of human responsibility. Men and women exercise their responsibility in society and culture by discerning, interpreting, and applying creational norms for the conduct of their lives. The precise form a societal institution takes in a given time or place is the result of how those who bear the responsibility understand the norm for that institution. Church elders, who put into practice the norm for the institutional church, work differently in Africa than in Europe, in the fourth century than in the twentieth century, in southern black churches than in northern white churches. Parents put a specific normative structure into practice for the family, corporate boards for corporations, parliaments or kings for states, school boards for schools, and so on. In each case, the authorities in a societal structure are responsible for implementing the norm.

An important principle emerges from this creationally oriented conception of the social order. The responsibility of the authorities in a given societal institution is *defined by its normative structure*. That is to say, the unique creational nature of the family, state, school, and the like specifies and delimits the authority exercised in each case. A father's authority is parental; it is both characterized and restricted by the peculiar nature of the family. The father is therefore obligated to exercise his authority in a distinctly familial way, not in a manner appropriate to, say, the police force or a hockey club. Ruling a family like a military unit, as the widowed father in *The Sound of Music* attempts to do, goes against the creationally established grain of the family. Conversely, a father qua father has no authority in, say, the school or the corporation. Likewise, the church elder's responsibility and authority is appropriate in the institutional church, but as an elder he must not act like a father to his congregation, either by ruling it in a "familial" or "paternalistic" manner or by intruding upon a father's sphere of responsibility in his congregation. The creational nature of the ecclesiastical institution must guide him in his official activities. The same principle holds for the authority of the business executive, the educator, the police officer, and so forth. All have an authority proper to their own sphere, which that sphere's creational structure defines and restricts.

The upshot of this principle—which Abraham Kuyper called "sphere sovereignty" but which we may also call the principle of "differentiated responsibility"—is that no societal institution is subordinate to any other. Persons in positions of societal authority (or "office") are called to positivize God's ordinances directly in their own specific sphere. Their authority is delegated to them by God, not by any human authority. Consequently, they are also directly responsible to God. Church, marriage, family, corporation, state, and school all stand *alongside* each other before the face of God. If one institution raises itself to a position of authority *over* the others, inserting its authority between that of God and the others, a form of totalitarianism emerges that violates the limited nature of each societal sphere. Such is the case in totalitarian states, in which political authority overrides all other authority. There the state runs the economic institutions, appoints church officials, and dictates child-rearing practices. Totalitarianism also characterized medieval Christendom; the institutional church spread its wings over the whole of European society, extending its ecclesiastical authority over education, family, business, and the state. Moreover, totalitarianism threatens to become the mark of contemporary society, in which the economic authority of certain vast transnational companies has become so extensive that in certain cases it interferes with the political sovereignty of states and with the spheres of many less powerful societal institutions.

Totalitarianism of whatever form is the directional perversion of the creational structures of society. The Christian is called to oppose all totalitarianism, whether of the state, church, or corporation, because it always signifies a transgression of God's mandated societal boundaries and an invasion into alien spheres. Perversion of God's creational design for society can occur in two ways: either through perversion of the norms within a given sphere (as in cases of injustice in the state, child abuse in the family, exploitative wages in the business enterprise) or through the extension of the authority of one sphere over another. In both cases Christians must oppose these distortions of God's handiwork. But that opposition should always *affirm* the proper and right exercise of responsibility. Political totalitarianism, for example, should be opposed not by rejecting the state as such (the error of anarchism) but by calling the state back to its God-ordained task of administering public justice. Christians should not simply lament the erosion of the family, for example, but should advocate measures enabling it to play its vital role once again. Not only must they confront exploitative corporations with the challenge of a normative view of the enterprise, but they must also enact legislation that both outlaws glaring cases of corporate abuse (against the environment, for example) and offers incentives for reassuming genuine corporate *responsibility*. Christians should actively engage in efforts to make every societal institution assume its own responsibility, warding off the interference of others. That, too, is participation in the restoration of creation and the coming of the kingdom of God.

Personal Renewal

Aggression. Thus far we have applied the structure-direction distinction very broadly, to society at large. It may be useful at this point to focus our attention on something closer to our personal lives: our emotions. Certainly our emotions are personal and also very important. It will profit us to consider how different worldviews have evaluated human emotions, and specifically how Greek disdain for the "passions" has affected the Christian church. For our purposes it will be valuable to focus on one aspect of human emotion—*aggression*.

In general, people consider aggressive behavior (which includes anger, competition, and self-assertion) to be either bad or good. This inclination is particularly evident among Christians. On the one hand, some believers condemn all evidence of aggression as conflicting with the biblical ideals of gentleness and meekness and with the central command of love. To stand up for yourself, to insist on a certain course of action, to fight hard to win in sports or succeed in business are at best tolerated. And many who disapprove of aggression in this way have corresponding feelings of guilt whenever they do express anger or behave aggressively. Moreover, those who view aggression with suspicion tend to feel the same way about human emotion in general, and strive for suppression and control rather than free and open expression. They consider aggression to be an essentially sinful phenomenon, a result of the fall and not a part of the good created order. After all, did not Jesus himself relate anger to the commandment against murder (Matt. 5:22), and did not Paul list "wrath" among the works of the flesh (Gal. 5:20, KJV)? A Christian psychotherapy founded on this view seeks to bring the client to the point where the need for anger and assertiveness is no longer felt.

On the other hand, some Christians see aggression as a natural human function that is essential to emotional health. Drawing on the work of such ethologists as Konrad Lorenz (whose book *On Aggression* has become something of a classic), they point out how aggressive behavior plays a very positive role in the animal world, where it serves to ensure the survival of the species. They argue that human beings too have a natural instinct for aggression that should not be obstructed. If it is blocked, they say, all kinds of neuroses and emotional maladjustments might result. These Christians go so far as to encourage aggressive behavior, suggesting at the same time that aggression should be channeled through socially acceptable outlets or expressed in settings in which it does not damage those against whom it is directed. Psychotherapists of this persuasion, many Christians included, encourage their clients to express their anger, to stand up for themselves when dealing with other people. They may even recommend assertiveness training to help them channel their aggression.

Clearly, these different approaches contradict each other. What one school of thought diagnoses as the ailment, the other recommends as the cure. And yet sincere and committed Christians stand on each side of the issue. A biblical worldview enables us to avoid this false dilemma. It helps us to formulate the problem differently, and in so doing it helps to provide us with a genuinely effective means to deal practically with our feelings. Often the way a question is posed determines the answer (or the range of possible answers) to that question. In the case of aggression, the implicit question shared by both parties in the debate is this: "Is aggression good or bad?" This question permits only two answers, and since those two answers are only half right, they are at best misleading and at worst downright false.

If we phrase the question in terms of the structure-direction distinction, then the question becomes, "In aggression, what is structural and what is directional?" Now the possible answers are much different. Underlying our query is the assumption that the fundamental biblical realities of creation, fall, and redemption apply here as elsewhere. Aggression must therefore involve features both of our created human nature and of the perversion or (at least potential) sanctification and restoration of that nature in Jesus Christ. A Christian analysis approaching the question about aggression in such terms can easily take into account the ethological data collected by Lorenz and his followers as well as honor the scriptural texts that repeatedly warn against sinful anger and strife and that ascribe wrath to God and zeal to his servants.

A few Christian psychologists have explicitly analyzed aggression in terms of structure and direction. In an article entitled "Love and Aggression," Dr. Harry Van Belle makes the point that "aggression is a created part of human life. It belongs to the structure of being human that we are aggressive with each other." He points out that an element of aggressiveness is essential to a good discussion, to healthy competition and games, to taking initiative in a leadership role, to pursuing a loved one, and even to making love. Moreover, Van Belle argues that aggression is often called for in response to sin, as in admonition and righteous indignation. "The opposite of love is not aggression but hate," he writes. "Aggression can be the loving thing to do, and only becomes the opposite of love as hateful aggression."

Hateful aggression is the perversion of a good creational gift. To oppose it is to oppose not the gift but the perversion. The call for Christians, therefore, is to *sanctify* aggression, not to *repress* it. Meekness and aggression need not be contradictory. Paul tells Timothy that the Lord's servant must be kind and forbearing, "in meekness *correcting* them that oppose themselves" (2 Tim. 2:25, ASV). There the verb translated "correct" (*paideuein*)—normally rendered "chasten" or "chastize"—has a strongly aggressive connotation.

Christians may then acknowledge that the work of Lorenz and other ethologists brings genuine insight into creational states of affairs on the point of aggression. But Lorenz fails to recognize that aggression, especially in humankind, is caught in the religious antithesis. There are real distinctions of good and evil in aggression. The original title of Lorenz's *On Aggression* is very telling in this regard; he called it *Das sogenannte Böse* ("so-called evil") to highlight his claim that what we normally call evil is simply the manifestation of the good and natural aggression drive. We need not accept Lorenz's elimination of *direction* in human aggression to learn from him concerning its creational *structure*. Seen in that light, aggression is one further instance of something created by God that should not be rejected but "sanctified by the word of God and prayer" (1 Tim. 4:5).

Spiritual Gifts. It may seem a big jump to move from aggression to the charismatic gifts, the gifts of the Holy Spirit. There are similarities between the two, however, if only because both are closely tied to human emotion, and because the discrimination of structure and direction is as helpful in the one case as it is in the other. Unfortunately, they are also similar in the extent to which opinion concerning them has polarized, though the controversy is even more intense in the case of spiritual gifts.

Normally, people mean by the "gifts" such extraordinary abilities as speaking in tongues, prophesying, and healing. Paul describes them with the word *charismata*, "free gifts" (1 Cor. 12). Today there are two extreme positions regarding these abilities. One is that they are supernatural gifts intrinsically superior to more ordinary gifts such as patience and kindness, and that the Christian who possesses them has a higher spiritual status. The other extreme holds that all contemporary manifestations of the charismatic gifts are at best an oddity and at worst a fake. Speaking in tongues, for example, is considered a strange kind of ecstatic utterance that is neither supernatural nor even uniquely Christian. As a "natural" phenomenon, it fits within the range of traditional psychological categories. The same applies to the gifts of healing and prophecy: no supernatural agency is needed to explain these extraordinary abilities.

Before we analyze these conflicting viewpoints, it may be well to look carefully at the word *supernatural*, which occurs so often in discussions of the spiritual gifts. The term has a number of different meanings, all of which involve the idea that "nature" is transcended. *Nature* may mean "creation" (in which case only God and his acts are supernatural) or "earthly creation (in which case God and heavenly creatures are supernatural) or "the secular realm" (in which case the church and Christian virtues are supernatural). Moreover, *supernatural* can be understood to apply not only to something that itself transcends "nature" (however defined) but also to something that belongs to "nature" but owes its existence to some extraordinary power or influence outside nature. I consider the fruits of the Spirit as "supernatural" in this last sense, not in the sense that they transcend created reality.

If we take *supernatural* to mean "above earthly creation," then I believe on the basis of the structure-direction distinction that the charismatic gifts are not supernatural at all; rather, they belong to the nature of God's good created earth. They are gifts of the Spirit as genuinely as love, joy, and peace are, but they do not add anything to what God had intended for his earthly creation from the beginning. They are therefore thoroughly "natural." They are like faith: only someone regenerated by the Spirit can have faith (true faith, that is, faith in Jesus Christ), but this regeneration does not make that faith foreign to the Creator's original purpose. And just as faith as a general human function is not unknown outside the body of Christ (though it is always misdirected there), so the charismatic gifts are not unknown outside Christianity (though they are misdirected and abused there). As creational possibilities, the *charismata* manifest structural traits; as serving either the kingdom of God or the world, they manifest directional traits.

The importance of this point is that spiritual gifts are fundamentally on a par with all other gifts. More correctly, all human gifts opened up by the Spirit of God for the edification of the church and the coming of his kingdom are by that token *spiritual* gifts. The gift of tongues is a great and glorious gift of God (if used appropriately), but the same is true of, say, the gift of intelligence (with the same proviso) and the gift of administration. In fact, Paul expressly mentions administration as a *charisma* in 1 Corinthians 12:28. Peter uses the same word when talking about such "ordinary" gifts as extending hospitality and "serving" (probably to be understood as waiting on tables) in 1 Peter 4:9-11. All human talents and abilities can flourish and blossom under the regenerating and sanctifying influence of the Holy Spirit to the glory and service of God. When opened up by the Spirit they are all charismatic gifts. This applies to social tact, to a way with children, to a knack for communicating, to mechanical skill, or whatever. There may be degrees of importance or splendor in the gifts, but all alike qualify as "charismatic" and "spiritual" if they are directed to Christ's redemption, sanctification, and reconciliation.

This is not to say that everyone has the potential to possess all the charismatic gifts, including tongue-speaking and healing. Certainly we cannot all possess all of them to the same degree. Just as we do not all have a natural head for figures or a talent for administration, no matter how saintly or well-coached we may be, so we can assume that not everyone is naturally gifted with the more dramatic of the charismatic gifts. On the other hand, the gifts may be much more widely distributed than we presently suspect. The point for now is simply that they are not supernatural—that is, they are not foreign to the everyday reality God created for us.

This position is neither a put-down of the gifts nor a sellout to irrational enthusiasm. It is rather a refusal to accept the current dilemma and an effort to make the biblical distinction between creation and the claims of Satan and Christ upon it fruitful for Christian insight. We must all seek to develop the gifts that God has given us, not forgetting that the greatest of these is love.

Sexuality. Another issue, a very sensitive one, around which opinion has polarized in our society is human sexuality. Here too we find that extreme positions have affected the thinking of the Christian community and that it is necessary to break through false dilemmas.

On the one side we find the view (often misrepresented as *the* traditional Christian position) that sex is essentially bad and should be avoided as much as possible. Some believe that though it may be necessary for the perpetuation of the human race, it is merely a necessary evil, that one should not take pleasure in sex, and certainly that the biblical teaching of sanctification does not apply to it. This negative attitude toward sex, which expresses itself in prudishness, taboos, and repression, is often designated (somewhat unfairly) as "puritan" or (with greater justification) as "Victorian." Certainly such an attitude is not very biblical.

On the other side we find a glorification of sex as the road to true meaning and self-fulfillment. In reaction to the Victorian view, much of Western civilization has during the past few decades come to view sexuality as an unqualified good. It is argued that sexual relations, whether within marriage or outside of it, whether heterosexual or homosexual, whether rooted in genuine caring or not, are intrinsically and unqualifiedly beneficial. Breaking the traditional standards is considered liberating. Sexuality is held to be a basic and natural drive, and if this drive is frustrated, the cost is debilitating neurosis and inhibition.

As is typical with this type of polarization, each side in the discussion is only half right and is therefore seriously misleading. Christians who believe themselves to be confronted with the choice of either maligning or glorifying human sexuality often enough make the serious mistake of attempting to find a "middle road," an ethical golden mean that avoids the extremes of both emphases. But the challenge for Christians is to break through the false dilemma giving rise to the extremes. Once more, the question is not "Is sexuality basically good or bad?" but rather "What is structural and what is directional about human sexuality?" If structure and direction are the terms of reference, it then becomes possible both to *affirm* human sexuality wholeheartedly and to *oppose* its perversions with equal conviction and vigor.

Lewis B. Smedes's book *Sex for Christians* provides a useful discussion of sexuality in these terms. It explicitly puts sexuality in the context of the biblical themes of creation, fall, and redemption and thus implicitly applies the structure-direction distinction. Smedes notes that the first part of the book "is about human sexuality—in its created goodness, its sinful distortions, and its redeemed potential." This is reflected in the headings of the chapters that deal with these three aspects: "Let Us Rejoice and Be Glad in It," "Distorted Sexuality," and "Salvation and Sexuality." Smedes's expression of this thoroughly biblical perspective is succinct and incisive:

> Grace does not destroy nature: neither does it despise what God has made. Creation and grace are together in God's mind. *Redemption restores what we have corrupted and distorted, including what we have distorted in our sexuality.* But redemption does not turn us from sexuality; it illumines the goodness of it. (P. 104; emphasis added)

Or, as he goes on to say, "The discovery of grace is the discovery of creation's goodness as well as the discovery of sin's badness." To restate this in the vocabulary we have been using, grace in Jesus Christ opens our eyes to both structure and direction.

But what is structural and what is directional in sexuality—what is God's creational design for sex and what are the perversions that we must overcome through the power of the Spirit? This is not an easy question to answer. To be sure, the Scriptures are plain enough about some essential points: God designed human sexuality for the context of heterosexual marriage and committed human love; deviations from this (bestiality, homosexual relations, adultery, prostitution, loveless lust) are all roundly condemned. But what about such matters as petting, masturbation, and sexual fantasies? The Bible does not explicitly address these issues, leaving them instead to the Spirit-led good judgment of Christians. They lie in ethical grey areas where spiritual discernment and mature insight into human nature must play the decisive role.

The difficulty of discerning creational revelation in certain situations raises two general points that we must bear in mind when applying the structure-direction distinction to a given phenomenon, whatever it may be. The first was indicated already in our discussion of creation: when attempting to discern what the normative patterns of creation are, Scripture—the architect's verbal explanation of his blueprint—is our first and indispensable guide. The data of social psychology do not tell us, for example, that the Creator did not intend that we should engage in extramarital sex. Although the creation order instills some awareness in most cultures of the normative connection between sexuality and marriage, we still need the Scriptures to make this link unambiguous. Only with the corrective lens of Scripture can we discern what is normative in the tangled mass of psychological and sociological data on sexual mores in different cultures. The same holds true for discerning the distorted character of bestiality and homosexuality. Though the creational blueprint is perhaps more easily read in this connection, nevertheless, without clearly spelled out authoritative directives in human language, even a society like that of the highly cultured ancient Grees (including the philosophers Socrates and Plato) could look upon homosexuality as a normal part of the natural scheme of things. The Greek perception of the structure of human sexuality was seriously distorted because it lacked the light of Scripture.

Our second point concerns the uncertainties and ambiguities that often beset an interpretation of creation in areas where the Scriptures give no explicit or detailed directives. As we indicated in the discussion of creation, this problem parallels that of personal "guidance" or "calling." There are no easy or readily agreed upon answers in these areas, though certainly there are answers to be found. My point in this connection is simply that the fruitfulness of the structure-direction distinction lies not so much in giving *answers* (easy or otherwise) as in suggesting biblically based *questions*. Structure-direction is not an easy formula for producing the right Christian solution to perplexing cultural or ethical problems; instead, it provides an avenue of attack, a line of research, a way of probing the issue geared to the Creator's revealed perspective on things.

In the fuzzy area of sexual ethics, therefore, we should not give up searching for the path that the Lord wants us to walk, nor should we declare that the issues involved are ethically indifferent or neutral. Our guidelines should be the general teachings of Scripture (e.g., creation, fall, redemption), the specific biblical directives for the area of sexuality (e.g., its heterosexual design), and the evidence of experience gained by a wisdom rooted in the fear of the Lord (such evidence may well include the findings of scientific research). Given these guidelines, the Christian must seek out the Lord's way by exercising spiritual discernment within the communal context of the body of Christ. Like all searching, this quest may involve a measure of trial and error, but here too we must work out our salvation in fear and trembling, knowing that it is indeed God who works in us to will and act according to his good purpose.

Suppose we apply this approach to the issue of sexual fantasy. It seems fair to say that imagination as such is an excellent part of God's handiwork, as is the enjoyment we derive from looking at an attractive member of the opposite sex. In themselves, these gifts are part of the good creation of God, "who richly provides us with everything for our enjoyment" (1 Tim. 6:17). They belong to our creational makeup. At the same time, Christ teaches that the seventh commandment is directed not only against extramarital sex but also (in the case of men) against "looking on a woman to lust after her" (Matt. 5:27, KJV). It is possible, in fact, to commit adultery in the heart. Imagination, too, is easily perverted by sin and needs the renewal made possible in Jesus Christ. As in everything, it is precisely in and through their struggle *against* the work of Satan that Christians are challenged to engage their willing and doing *for* the work of God in their lives. Sexual fantasies, too, must be sanctified. It is high time that the Christian community begin a reflection on an ethics of the imagination, a reflection based on the creational goodness and structure of the imagination and on an awareness of how sin and grace affect that imagination.

Human sexuality, a part of God's good creation, ought to be affirmed and accepted with thanksgiving. To be sure, sexual perversion (of whatver kind) must be combatted vigorously—the Scriptures are unmistakable on this score—but the battle should be waged only with a view to creational *affirmation*. Sexual immorality should be opposed not to repress sex but to show forth its true glory. Scrubbing a linen garment to remove accumulated dirt may seem like a negative activity, but with respect to the beauty of the garment itself it is in reality positive. Redeemed sexuality participates in the beauty of holiness and therefore may be fully enjoyed and celebrated to God's glory.

Dance. In some ways dance is closely related to the question of sexuality. Many Christian traditions have developed a negative attitude toward social dancing if not toward ballet and folk dances. This attitude has certainly characterized the churches that follow the line of Calvin, who himself roundly condemned dance on the grounds that it arouses passion and invites promiscuity.

One Calvinistic denomination that for most of its history took a negative view of dance is the Christian Reformed Church in North America, of which I am a member. Within our circles dancing was long considered simply a "worldly amusement" and was therefore strictly prohibited. The Christian Reformed Church has recently modified its official position, however, on the basis of an excellent denominational report (entitled "Dance and the Christian Life") that works explicitly with the creation-fall-redemption worldview. Although the report does not use the terms *structure* and *direction*, it does nevertheless use these concepts to break through the unhealthy dilemma between "worldliness" and "unworldliness" with respect to dance.

The report correctly poses the issue as follows:

> We need to sort out (1) what there is about the dance that goes back to creation and thus reflects a gift of God, (2) what the impact of our fallen condition is on dancing, and (3) if and how Christians may seek to redeem this area of life. Unless we keep these questions in mind we continually run the risk of condemning the legitimate in our zeal to reject evil, or of embracing the corrupt in our desire to do justice to the good. We are always in danger of rejecting the creational in the name of the fall, and of accepting the fallen in the name of creation.

Putting it in the terminology we have been using, we might say that the distinction between structure and direction is necessary for avoiding the false arguments that so often bedevil Christian thinking on this topic. What is structural about dancing? At first glance, almost the whole of it. Bodily movement is clearly part of God's good creation, as is rhythm, music, and social interaction. The Creator gave us the good gift of bringing these together for celebration and enjoyment, as we know from the many biblical references to dancing. Nor would it seem that there is anything anticreational about two people dancing together, since celebration is social by nature. As such, dancing would seem to be a beautiful, healthy, enjoyable, and exhilarating experience, for which we may thank God.

But there is little if anything that humankind cannot corrupt, and dance is certainly not exempt from the impact of human sin. In modern social dancing the distortion of dance becomes most obvious when it becomes the occasion, or the intended means, for sexual arousal, or aggression, or promiscuity. This is not to suggest that a sexual element in dancing is evil, any more than the presence of sexuality is evil in clothing, sports, or drama. But when the element of sexual attraction, which is a legitimate and pleasing undertone of all normal social relations between the sexes, is the dominant focus, then social dancing becomes the kind of sexual foreplay that is appropriate only to marriage. Reinforced by provocative dress, suggestive music or lyrics, hypnotic lighting, and liquor or drugs, this type of dancing is positively pagan. The element of deliberate sexual suggestiveness or provocation is also present in more genteel and refined forms of social dancing. It was this perversion of the good gift of dancing that led Christian thinkers such as Calvin to reject it altogether.

A certain cultural phenomenon may be so terribly and thoroughly distorted in a given historical setting that it is a matter of Christian wisdom to avoid it altogether. The profession of acting at the time of the early church is one such example. By the third century A.D., the time of the church father Cyprian, the Roman stage had become so thoroughly corrupt (sexual intercourse was a regular part of the program), that all professional actors who became Christians were compelled to abandon their profession. It may be that in our society certain forms of dance have become so intimately tied to cultural expressions of hedonism that Christians ought to recoil from them entirely. Nevertheless, we should not reject dancing as such, for the dance continues to participate in the creational goodness of God. Everything created by God is good and is reclaimed by Jesus Christ. The question is not "Does this belong to Christ too?" The question is rather "What is the most effective manner of bringing reformation and sanctification to this area of our lives?"

Some relatively straightforward guidelines to this question might include the following. Avoid dancing in a setting that is "worldly" in the sense of being dominated by service of Satan rather than service by of Christ. Give explicit attention in the choice of dance steps, music, and lyrics to the possibilities of honoring God. Commission sensitive and gifted Christian dancers to demonstrate and teach experimental dance styles inspired by the principle of Christian reformation. Form study and discussion groups on the history of dance and on the good and bad features of contemporary dances. Develop alternatives to male-female partnering in social dancing. Finally, explore the possibilities of liturgical dance as a way to appreciate the positive potential of dance.

All these suggestions are examples of how Christians can learn to discern structure and direction in dance in order to combat sickness and affirm health. The Lord of all creation is also the Lord of the dance, and the kingdom of God will not come in its fullness without the redemption of this area of human celebration and enjoyment also.

Conclusion

It would not be difficult to multiply the examples of problems or issues in contemporary culture that can be approached from a distinctively biblical slant by bringing to bear the categories of structure and direction. Technology and education, for instance, come readily to mind.

It bears repeating, in concluding this little book, that a biblical worldview does not provide answers, or even a recipe for finding answers, to the majority of perplexing problems with which our culture confronts us today. What it does is provide a way of framing the question, to give what German thinkers like to call a *Problemstellung*, that is distinct and peculiarly biblical. To approach the phenomena of the world in terms of structure and direction is to look at reality through the corrective lens of Scripture, which everywhere speaks of a good creation and the drama of its reclamation by the Creator in Jesus Christ. It is precisely these two themes, which establish the worldview foundation of genuine biblical thinking, that have been denied or marginalized in the dominant tradition of humanism that has shaped Western civilization since the Renaissance. A recovery of this dual emphasis in Scripture—in a word, cosmic re-creation in Christ—as the foundation of our Christian analysis and reflection can help us to look with fresh eyes at a world we have been conditioned to interpret in humanistic categories. Such a fresh look does not provide easy answers, but it does provide a well-founded hope of *sound* answers once the appropriate work of careful observation and hard thinking has been undertaken.

Scripture does not provide a shortcut to circumvent research and analysis, but it does set authoritative, foundational parameters in terms of which such research and analysis can be done with profit.

A final word needs to be said about the relationship of worldview to philosophy. This is a theme that carries our discussion into the realm of theoretical inquiry and the scientific enterprise. If a world-view is to have real academic bite to it—that is to say, if the basic categories of a given worldview are to become effective and opera-tional in the doing of science (understood in the broad sense of the German *Wissenschaft*, embracing the humanities as well as the social and natural sciences)—it must leave its mark on the elaboration of specifically philosophical categories. All academic disciplines are confronted, on the foundational level, with issues of a philosophical nature (e.g., the status of universals, the problem of freedom and determinism, the justification of belief, etc.). The answers that sci-entists give, implicitly or explicitly, to such issues depend on phil-osophical categories that are themselves decisively shaped by a deeper-lying worldview. There is therefore an influence of worldview on scholarship via the mediation of philosophical categories.

This is a very large claim to make, and it falls outside the limits of this book to explain and defend it. My concern here is simply to point out that the reformational worldview we have been consid-ering itself calls for a reformational philosophy that can relate the basic insights of a biblical perspective to the groundwork of a sys-tematic philosophy that is relevant to the special disciplines of the university. I am thinking, for example, of the reformational philos-ophy of the Dutch thinkers D. H. T. Vollenhoven and Herman Dooyeweerd, each of whom (in his own way) sought to develop a Christian philosophy on the basis of a biblical worldview, and thus to provide the beginnings of a Christian reformation of the entire scientific enterprise. In a sense, this book is meant as an introduc-tion to such a philosophy and to such a program of academic renewal.

But academics, including philosophy, is only one area in the broad expanse of God's creation, and it is not only those who teach and learn at universities who can profit from explicit reflection on the world perspective that the gospel brings. All thoughtful Chris-tians, in whatever area they are called to exercise their responsibilities, must take seriously the question of biblcal worldview, and must guide both their thinking and their acting accordingly. To ignore the question is to deny the practical relevance of Scripture to the greater part of our workaday lives.